GOD
and
EVIL

GOD
AND
EVIL

Studies in the Mystery of
Suffering and Pain

by WILLIAM FITCH

LONDON
PICKERING & INGLIS LTD.

PICKERING & INGLIS LTD.
29 LUDGATE HILL, LONDON, E.C.4
26 BOTHWELL STREET, GLASGOW, C.2

Printed in Great Britain by Lowe & Brydone (Printers) Ltd., London

CONTENTS

CHAPTER ONE

PRELUDE

No canonical writer has ever used Nature to prove God.
Pascal, *Pensées*, IV, 243

I said: "Let me walk in the fields."
  He said: "No, walk in the town."
I said: "There are no flowers there."
  He said: "No flowers, but a crown."

I said: "But the air is thick,
  And fogs are veiling the sun."
He answered: "Yet souls are sick,
  And souls in the dark undone."

I cast one look at the fields,
  Then set my face to the town;
He said, "My child, do you yield?
  Will you leave the flowers for a crown?"

Then into His hand went mine,
  And into my heart came He;
And I walk in a light divine,
  The path I had feared to see.

George MacDonald, *Obedience*

His sense of the human tragedy fortified him against self-deception and easy consolation.

John F. Kennedy, speaking about Robert Frost

IT WAS TWO O'CLOCK in the morning. We had been talking a long time. The fire in the grate had burned low but still the questions kept coming.

"If, as you say, God is sovereign and good, then why does He allow these things to happen?"

One of us, I don't recall who, drowsily muttered Francis Thompson's lines,

> Nothing begins, and nothing ends, that is not paid with
> a moan;
> For we are born in others' pain, and perish in our own.

"And it all seems so meaningless," he went on. "Why, think of it! Every form of life lives by preying on another. Think of the pain that animals suffer! How can you believe in God when these things happen?"

Someone else interjected,

> Same old slippers, same old rice,
> Same old glimpse of Paradise.

"But you know something," he added, "I wish I could believe that somewhere there could be an answer. I used to believe . . . but since coming here I've lost it all. I read Matthew Arnold the other night, and he seemed to be saying what I'm thinking these days:

> The sea of faith
> Was once, too, at the full, and round earth's shore
> Lay like the folds of a bright girdle furled;
> But now I only hear
> Its melancholy, long, withdrawing roar,
> Retreating, to the breath
> Of the night-wind, down the vast edges drear
> And naked shingles of the world.

There was silence for a while. The silence of thought. "Why should there be bacteria, earthquakes, droughts, famine? And why should there be ghettos and segregation, hydrogen bombs and Hiroshimas — exploitation and intimidation, brainwashings and torture chambers?"

"And why doesn't your God do something about it all?"

This is where this book began. The discussion had started quite spontaneously after supper. It soon went to the roots too. "Is evil a basic element in reality? Or an aberration of some kind? A sort of malfunction in an otherwise good universe?"

"Is man responsible for the evil in the world? Why do so many bad people escape trouble completely? And why do so many good people suffer? What has your Christianity to say to these things?"

I recalled and quoted a sentence of C. S. Lewis: "God whispers to us in our pleasures, speaks in our conscience, but shouts in our pains; suffering is His megaphone to rouse a deaf world." And I went on, thinking out loud in some such words as these: "If there were no human avarice, there would be no exploiting of the poor. If there were no selfishness, we wouldn't be troubled with power-hungry men or nations. But the Bible is all about this very issue of God and evil. Moral evil is never covered up in the Bible. And the whole question of suffering is discussed in the book of Job. The Bible holds that nothing happens by chance and that God has His plan for all history. Let's discover the Bible's answer to the whole tragic dilemma of evil — let's study it together."

For more than two months we studied the biblical answers to God and evil. The chapters here presented are based on the conviction that the Bible is wholly trustworthy and that on this tremendous question it reveals the mind and heart of the God who made us all. For me, the Bible is an authoritative book. I did not come to this position lightly or easily. But experience has proved it to be a book of life, containing the whole counsel of God for man's salvation and deliverance from evil.

CHAPTER TWO

THE SOVEREIGNTY
OF GOD — AND EVIL

God, the great Creator of all things, doth uphold, direct, dispose, and govern all creatures, actions and things, from the greatest even to the least, by His most wise and holy providence, according to His infallible foreknowledge, and the free and immutable counsel of His own will, to the praise of the glory of His wisdom, power, justice, goodness, and mercy.

Westminster Confession of Faith, Chapter Five

THE FIRST QUESTION which must be faced comes when we confront the fact of the sovereignty of God and the fact of evil. If God is good and if God is absolutely sovereign in power, then why is there any evil in the world at all? Can He not by one great sweep of His hand erase evil completely from His creation?

To discover the biblical position on this question we could go to many different parts of the Bible. There is no one passage, however, to compare with Isaiah's tremendous chapter — the forty-fifth — in which he deals with the sovereignty of God in thoughts and language that have never been equalled. At the same time, he faces squarely the basic question which is before us now: Who is responsible for the evil in the world, and is there any escape from it? "I am the Lord, and there is none else," God says through the inspired lips of His prophet. He is addressing Cyrus, the conquering king through whom the chosen people are to be delivered from Babylonian bondage, and He goes on to say to him, "I girded thee, though thou hast not known me. There is no God besides me: I am the Lord, and there is none else."[1] This God repeats; and He does so to signify that this is a

[1]Is. 45:5. All quotations of Scripture are from the King James version unless otherwise noted.

truth which all men must be made to hear. "That they may know from the rising of the sun, and from the west, that there is none besides me. I am the Lord, and there is none else."[2] The theme develops yet more firmly. "I have made the earth, and created man upon it: I, even my hands, have stretched out the heavens, and all their host have I commanded."[3] This theme is repeated in varying ways until the climax of the whole is reached in the words: "Look unto me, and be ye saved, all the ends of the earth: for I am God, and there is none else."[4] God rules and reigns. God is sovereign. That is the word that the prophet is given to proclaim to all men everywhere.

At the heart of these majestic words of prophecy there is a verse in which *the problem of evil is faced in the light of the divine sovereignty*. God speaks again through His servant and says: "I am the Lord, and there is none else. I form the light, and [I] create darkness: I make peace, and [I] create evil: I the Lord do all these things."[5] Nothing could be more definite than that. Here is a word of the Holy Spirit that faces the issue directly and answers it as fully as our minds can understand the mind and will of God. "I create darkness . . . I create evil." In these words God accepts responsibility for the presence of evil in the midst of His creation; and this is a revelation which we dare not lightly dismiss nor try to explain away.

God is sovereign. That is Isaiah's theme. It is the theme of all the Bible, but here it finds its clearest and noblest expression. There is one God and He is over all. The attributes of God are of course manifold. To think rightly about God we must think of His eternity, omniscience, omnipotence, omnipresence, faithfulness, goodness, holiness, justice, mercy and grace. Through all these attributes there shines His majesty. The living God is a

[2]Is. 45:6.   [4]Is. 45:22.
[3]Is. 45:12.   [5]Is. 45:6, 7.

sovereign God, sovereign over all the works of His hands, all-wise and absolutely free. Were God to be lacking in one iota of knowledge, freedom or power, He would not, He could not, be God. He, however, lacks nothing. "The Father hath life in himself."[6] That is how our Lord expresses this truth, and in saying so He outreaches the thoughts of mortal man. God's life is not a gift from another. He is Himself Life — an unfathomable sea of life and glory and blessedness. None can dictate to Him. None can compel Him nor stop Him. He requires permission from none to act or speak. He is the first and the last, and besides Him there is no god.

Of course, that is not the way that the natural man of the world thinks. When you read the daily papers, you don't find much of this kind of thinking. When you talk with men generally, you don't get much response if you turn the subject towards the sovereignty of God. It is much more likely that some kind of reply will be given about God being dead. God is not in the thinking of the normal man of our generation. Indeed, it may be truly said that this generation is unique in having no theological foundation at all to its thinking. The word "humanity" today commonly implies secularized man. Our age is, in Paul Tillich's apt phrase, "a land of broken symbols." Spiritual foundations have crumbled. Spiritual horizons are blurred if not non-existent. Society has been secularized. Our cities have become sophisticated, that is, they are increasingly characterized by the absence of theological signposts. A militant, secularistic world view dominates the press, politics both local and national, the world of business, and more and more our universities and schools of higher learning. This is a fact of life today and the Church must face it. The tragedy of it all is that the Church herself has capitulated to this atmosphere and no longer speaks

[6]John 5:26.

as Isaiah did. It is indeed very questionable whether the Church
really believes as Isaiah did in such a sovereign God — believes,
that is, with her heart and soul and mind and strength. She may
still give passing acknowledgment to the truth of a sovereign
God, but in the actual arena of life this has come to mean
nothing at all. The Church, too, has become secularized, worldly,
content to take out landed immigrant status in the world which
crucified her Lord, forgetful of the higher calling of her Lord.
No longer is she the pilgrim Church, looking for a city which
hath foundations, whose builder and maker is God. No! She is
too much at home where she is. God is not in all her thoughts
and the vision of the throne eternal and immortal has been almost totally obliterated.

We should not be altogether surprised at this. Our Lord has
forewarned us that thus it would be. He told His disciples that
the love of many would wax cold and that iniquity would
abound. He openly asked, "When the Son of man cometh, shall
he find faith on the earth?"[7] The people of God ought not to be
dismayed at what they see and hear. The pattern of world history
is developing exactly as our Lord has said it would. What is
needed is a voice to be heard speaking for God — declaring that
God is, and that He is sovereign over all. And this is the true
mission of the Church; she is summoned to tell out the good
news that God is love and that He lives to pour that love into
the lives of needy people everywhere. The Christian is commanded to lift up his voice and to say to the cities of the earth,
"Behold your God."[8] He is to declare that God is the sovereign
God of all history; that history begins and will end under God;
that the idols of the earth are mere wind and waste; that all the
Babylons of the earth will fall before Him when He comes to

[7]Luke 18:8.   [8]Is. 40:9.

judge the world in righteousness; and that no one will be able to stand on his own merits before Him when He appears.

This will not be popular preaching. It never has been. A self-sufficient world, run by self-sufficient men, a world where temporality is conclusive and final, a world that is more set on medicare than on finding the balm of Gilead to heal the sickness of its soul, a world bent upon gain rather than godliness, social security rather than salvation from sin, this kind of world will not readily accept such preaching. But if the Church is truly to be the Church of her Lord and Saviour Jesus Christ, she must not shrink from the Master's commission. She must declare the whole counsel of God, and that means proclaiming that God is over all and under all, and that to Him ultimately all men must give account of all they have done and thought and felt while here on earth.

But what about the problem of evil? It may even be accentuated by such wholehearted proclaiming of the sovereignty of God. How, and why, and to what purpose can a God of love have permitted evil? And if He is really omnipotent, why does He not remake everything far nearer to His heart's desire?

Let us turn to our key — in Isaiah, chapter 45 — and never let it go while we ask the questions we all must ask.

"I am the Lord, and there is none else," God says; and He adds, "I form the light, and [I] create darkness: I make peace, and [I] create evil: I the Lord do all these things." In these words the prophet, under the inspiration of the Holy Spirit, faces realistically the great question of the origin of evil. He does not try to evade the issue. He faces it directly and speaks with very great plainness of speech. "I create darkness . . . I create evil." This is the voice of God. This is divine revelation. What does it all mean?

We should first of all note what the words do not mean. The

Bible is its own interpreter, and we must understand the significance of any portion of the divine revelation in the light of every part of that revelation. Bearing this in mind, we can say very definitely that the words before us do not mean that God is the author of sin. God is holy, and in Him is no darkness at all. A sinless God, a God whose very nature is holiness, could not Himself produce sin. Nor can these words imply that God would ever entice a man to sin. "Let no man say," says James, "when he is tempted, I am tempted of God: for God cannot be tempted with evil, neither tempteth he any man: but every man is tempted, when he is drawn away of his own lust, and enticed."[9] When God says, "I create evil," He obviously does not imply that He at any time will try to tempt His creature to sin. Further, these words obviously cannot mean that God would ever design for evil an absolute part or place in His universe. The Bible ends with a portrayal of a reconstituted heaven and earth from which all evil has been swept away forever. The goal of divine redemption is consistently defined as one where sin will be vanquished and put away forevermore. The God of the Bible is a holy God, and He has made holiness the moral condition necessary to the spiritual health of the universe. This is the God and Father of our Lord and Saviour Jesus Christ, who knew no sin, who died to sin, and died for sinners. The God who sent His Son into the world to save sinners can under no circumstances, through no form of interpretation, nor by any stretch of the imagination, be considered as a God who could beget sin.

In what sense, then, is God the Creator of evil? When He says through His servant, "[I] create darkness ... [I] create evil," what does He mean? Is there any escape from the seeming illogicality of a sovereign God and the fact of evil? A complete ex-

[9]James 1:13, 14.

planation may elude our sinful finitude, but there are a few things which are revealed and which we must affirm.

I

The Bible tells us that God accepts responsibility for the presence of evil in His creation.

We may not be told all the reasons why this should be so, but it is clear that God was not caught off-guard when evil entered. It did so with His full cognizance, and God accepts responsibility for its presence and power among men.

The Bible knows nothing of any doctrine of dualism — any kind of belief in competing gods of equal power. That is how the sacred book of Zoroastrianism, loftiest of all non-biblical religions, gets round the difficulty of the fact of evil. It postulates two gods — Ormazd and Ahriman. Between them they created the world. The good god Ormazd created the good things; the evil Ahriman created all evil things. It was quite simple. There seemed to be no rivalry between them. They just made it so. But this is not Christian teaching. This is not biblical theology. The Bible knows of only one God — the living God, Father, Son and Holy Spirit. God's attributes are such as to make impossible the being or existence of another god. When the Zend-Avesta posits two gods, the Christian knows through the revelation of the Holy Scriptures that this is not true. "I am the Lord, and there is none else." Beyond that the Christian cannot go.

When God says, "I create evil," He accepts responsibility for evil in the midst of His creation. It is not enough to say, as Calvin does, that this evil refers to the evils of judgments and punishments which God sends upon men. The word that is used in this verse is *bara* — the word that is used in Genesis, chapter one, where we are told that "in the beginning God *created* the heaven and the earth"; "God *created* great whales, and every living creature that moveth"; "so God *created* man in his own image, in the image of God *created* he him; male and female *created* he them." The word *bara* is used here, as always, when the thought of absolute creation is being considered. We may contrast it with the verbs which are used with regard to "light" and "peace." "I form the light," "I make peace" — that is how God speaks when light and peace are discussed. There was no need for God to "create" either light or peace, for "God is light, and in him is no darkness at all,"[10] and the "fruit of the Spirit of God is peace."[11] God shares His own life with men when He gives to them the gift of light and peace. But evil is a different thing. It requires a special creation, and so the inspired Scriptures use the word *bara* — "I create evil."

Yet, saying so, we must add that in no sense does this imply that God is the author of evil. When God made man in His own image, He blessed him with the gift of self-determination, self-will, self-volition. He thus made man with a capacity of choice — a capacity therefore of choosing the good and turning from the evil. This must have been true also of angelic beings in aeons long before the creation of earth and of man upon it. We see things here only through a glass darkly. But whatever the facts may be as to the existence of evil prior to the creation of man — a subject which we shall discuss in detail when we consider Satan, the evil one — this much must be said here: God accepts responsibility for the presence of evil. Ultimately, though we see not yet the pattern of His way, evil will be made to be a means of glorifying God. God will raise from out of the world's evil heart His people, a people who will hate sin as He does and cleave unto righteousness and truth. But meanwhile we by faith accept the fact of evil as being accepted by God and as being

[10]I John 1:5.   [11]Gal. 5:22.

used by Him in some way that defies our mortal understanding to His everlasting glory.

II

The Bible also affirms that God restricts the operation of evil in His creation.

There is no point in all the Scriptures at which victory is conceded to the forces of darkness. Over and over again we hear the saints of God crying out, "How long, oh Lord, how long shall evil reign?" But even in their darkest hours, as out of the depths they cry to the throne above, the people of God are still confident that righteousness shall triumph and, ultimately, that love will reign. This is the confidence of the saints. All through the book of Revelation this is seen. The book deals with blood and martyrdom, the shattering of dreams, the mangling of the bodies of the people of God to exalt the pomp and pride of the Caesars. But even so there is no surrender to the dominion of evil. On the contrary! Flinging defiance at all the facts, the saints shout, "Babylon the great is fallen, is fallen."[12] Beyond the thrones of the emperors of Rome, they saw another throne and they worshipped another King. "The Lord God omnipotent reigneth."[13] This was their confidence. This was their peace.

In showing such substance to their faith, these early Christians are in exact focus with the whole Bible's testimony. For the Bible repeatedly emphasizes that God never suffers evil to get out of hand. He controls it; He restricts it. Satan is bound. He may have a long chain and be capable of doing untold hurt to multitudes, but his reign and rule are not absolute. He operates under sufferance. Evil is tolerated and restricted as a kind of fugitive outlaw whose activities are very definitely held in check and under the ceaseless surveillance of the eye of God.

[12]Rev. 18:2.   [13]Rev. 19:6.

God is working out a plan. The Bible calls it the plan of salvation. Like weak supporters of a strong-armed leader, people discover too late they are the slaves of an evil power. But God works outside the boundaries and within the enemy's bastions too. It is the purpose of God to redeem us from the power of evil and to ransom us from the thraldom of the evil one. This pattern also is plain. Often, when evil seems to be on the ascendant, God breaks in and makes the good to triumph. Were this not so, were there no plan of redemption, evil would indeed be unrestricted in its operation over all mankind. But, thank God, there is the plan of God — the plan of salvation. Thus, the Bible is far more than the story of man — the story of the rise and fall of kingdoms and empires — it is also the story of salvation. In "the determinate counsel and foreknowledge of God,"[14] this plan unfolds from generation to generation, and ultimately Christ is born to be the Saviour of the world and to "save his people from their sins."[15]

This is the thrilling optimism of biblical history. It is utterly realistic about evil but it never concedes victory to evil. The powers of evil are constricted. Their areas of operation are delineated and delimited by God. When Christ died upon the Cross, it seemed as though evil had really triumphed. But behold! — on the third day Christ rose from the dead. Satan and his legions are foiled and their basic weakness is exposed. And it is of this that Isaiah sings in this great Mount Everest chapter: "Drop down, ye heavens, from above, and let the skies pour down righteousness: let the earth open, and let them bring forth salvation, and let righteousness spring up together."[16] Here is biblical optimism at its highest and its best. God is not helpless amidst the seeming ruin of His creation. God is working His purposes out as year succeeds year; and His purposes are far beyond the understanding of mortal man. Yet this is clear. In that

[14]Acts 2:23.   [15]Matt. 1:21.   [16]Is. 45:8.

sovereign purpose, God will use evil to His glory. He will make the wrath of men to praise Him. He will not rest until evil has burned itself out and the whole creation is liberated into the glorious day when sin shall be no more.

III

We have seen that God accepts responsibility for the presence of evil and that He limits its range. Now hear God's promise. The Bible affirms that God will always provide a way of escape from evil.

God says, "I form the light" and "I make peace." God takes the initiative in providing a way of escape from the rule of evil. Of this Isaiah speaks in exultant lines: "Israel shall be saved in the Lord with an everlasting salvation.... For thus saith the Lord that created the heavens; God himself that formed the earth and made it; he hath established it, he created it not in vain, he formed it to be inhabited: I am the Lord, and there is none else. I have not spoken in secret, in a dark place of the earth: I said not unto the seed of Jacob, Seek ye me in vain: I the Lord speak righteousness: I declare things that are right."[17] Could anything more majestic, more comforting, more strengthening be spoken? The valley of tribulation may be very shadowed and dark; but in the midst of the valley God walks with His own and says, "When thou passest through the waters, I will be with thee."[18] His gift is light. His presence is peace.

All this was of course fulfilled in the fullness of time when Jesus came. He stood before men and cried, "I am the light of the world: he that followeth me shall not walk in darkness, but shall have the light of life."[19] He died upon the Cross, and by His death we may have "peace with God through our Lord

[17]Is. 45:17-19.   [18]Is. 43:2.   [19]John 8:12.

Jesus Christ."[20] At Calvary a fountain was opened for sin and for uncleanness, and there, from all the vileness of our sinful ways, we may be cleansed; and from all the power of indwelling sin we may be delivered by the power of the indwelling Spirit of God — the Spirit by whom our Saviour was raised in triumph from the grave. God provides this deliverance to all who seek it, to all who want it. "Sin shall not have dominion over you."[21] That is the promise of God. Evil need not reign any longer in our mortal minds and bodies because Christ has died and is risen again, and through Him there is final and complete deliverance from the bondage of sin. This is the good news of the Gospel of God's grace. He provides a way of escape from evil.

IV

There is one final note to be added. Isaiah in this great forty-fifth chapter of his prophecy reminds us that God calls all men to flee from the evil and to find in Him succour and strength.

This we see in verse 22. "Look unto me, and be ye saved, all the ends of the earth: for I am God, and there is none else." God is still on the throne. It is from His throne that He speaks. It is to His throne that we are summoned to look. It is a universal call, for God speaks to "the ends of the earth." This is not for some privileged élite. This is for all men. Evil need not be victorious for one single hour longer in the life of any man. But if he is to be delivered from the power of evil, man must look to God and cry to Him for mercy and for the grace of a mighty salvation. This God gives — to all who look to Him. It is here that we see His sovereignty most patently in operation. Without a single day's delay, we may put His sovereignty to the proof. We may test God and see if indeed it is true that He can deliver as He

[20]Rom. 5:1.   [21]Rom. 6:14.

says He can. Blessed are they that are prepared to put God thus to the test. They will not be disappointed.

From all the hardening powers of suffering and sorrow God will also set us free. From the bitterness that long-continued sickness may create, He can and does deliver. He can sanctify every cross that He calls us to bear. And He will never allow us to be tempted beyond our powers of endurance, for "with the temptation [He will] also make a way to escape, that [we] may be able to bear it."[22] This is the promise of the God who says, "I am the Lord, and there is none else." This is His word, the given word of the sovereign Creator of all. In the midst of darkness and at the heart of a world of evil, He sends the Light of Life and offers the blessing of the peace that passes all understanding.

[22] I Cor. 10:13.

CHAPTER THREE

THE TREE OF THE KNOWLEDGE OF GOOD AND EVIL

C

Adam was denied the tree of the knowledge of good and evil to test his obedience and prove that he was willingly under God's commands. The very name of the tree shows the sole purpose of the precept was to keep him content with his lot and to prevent him from becoming puffed up with wicked lust. But the promise by which he was bidden to hope for eternal life so long as he ate from the tree of life, and, conversely, the terrible threat of death once he tasted of the tree of the knowledge of good and evil, served to prove and exercise his faith. Hence it is not hard to deduce by what means Adam provoked God's wrath upon himself. Indeed, Augustine speaks rightly when he declares that pride was the beginning of all evils. For if ambition had not raised man higher than was meet and right, he could have remained in his original state.

Calvin, *Institutes of the Christian Religion* 2.1.4

In every age men have sought an answer to the origin of evil. Some have tried to explain it by explaining it away. Christian Science has given one of the most elaborate of these interpretations. Evil is only an illusion, it claims. Mrs. Mary Baker Eddy in her testament of faith — *Science and Health with Key to the Scriptures* — stresses this very greatly. She writes: "Evil has no reality. It is neither person, place nor thing, but is simply a belief, an illusion of material sense. Evil is a false belief, an illusion without real basis. If sin, sickness and death were understood as nothingness, they would soon disappear." This makes interesting reading. Unfortunately, even if the "evils" of sin and pain, sorrow and death, are not real, the illusion that they are real is very real. We land back therefore where we started. Evil is still with us — even though it be in an illusionary form.

Most men, however, recognize evil for what it is — an evil thing. Persistently they have asked the basic questions which are urged by such experience. What is evil? Is evil ultimately a basic element of reality? Or is evil an aberration of some kind, a malfunction of some part of an otherwise good universe? Where does evil come from? Is man responsible for the evil in him and around him? Or is he the sport and plaything of higher powers of evil? Are good and evil separable from one another? Or is it impossible really to know what is good without knowing at the same time what is evil? On top of these a host of other questions

31

come. Is man free to choose what is good? Or is he born with a fatal bias towards evil? and if so, can he be held accountable for this? Is evil the result of free will? And if so, why is it that there is no exception to the choice of the evil? Again, are physical evils the result of moral evil? If so, why is it that so many good men suffer while others, obviously evil, live apparently placid lives? What answer has the Bible to these insistent and provoking problems?

Many people have quoted these general statements on man, from Alexander Pope's *Essay on Man*:

> All *nature is but art, unknown to thee;*
> All *chance, direction, which thou canst not see;*
> All *discord, harmony not understood,*
> All *partial evil, universal good.*

But such a judgment is both superficial and unreal. Blandly to state that "partial evil" is really "universal good" will afford little comfort to a soldier blinded from the flaming heat of a napalm bomb, or to a mother helpless and too late, when her three-year-old daughter has fallen under the wheels of a two-ton truck. Some deeper explanation must be found.

The great religions of the world have all attempted some answer. Hinduism both in its classic and popular forms has taught that the evils men suffer today are the result of misdeeds in some previous existence. Blindness, bereavement, hunger, disaster and pain are all of them the merited punishments of the wrongs of a former life. This is the Hindu doctrine of Karma, and associated with it is the belief in the transmigration of souls, from which there is virtually no escape. It must be admitted that Hinduism does realistically face the "Why?" of evil; but the answer is one that gives no hope. In the revolving wheel of repeated existences there is only despair and no deliverance. How different from the Cross! By His suffering and passion Christ offers complete deliverance from all such speculation.

Buddhism rose as a religion in revolt against the doctrine of Karma in Hinduism. Buddha himself was born and lived the early part of his life as a Hindu. But the thought of the endless repetition of reincarnation became so distasteful to him, so contradictory and self-destroying, that he turned to a way of life in which evil could be forgotten and ignored. The answer to the problem of evil became for him the extinction of desire. To cultivate the death of desire became the ultimate of life. Evil resides in desire; and deliverance from evil must therefore lie in escape from or in death to desire. The answer of Buddhism to the problem of evil is the cultivation of such a death. Nirvana is really the extinction of all self-realization. Freedom from evil is obtainable only through the death of personality. Again how different is this from the Gospel of Christ! The inheritance Christ brings us is the discovery of true selfhood in the joy and service of His kingdom.

Islam has its answer, but its answer is also one that carries little hope with it. Evil, like good, comes as God dictates. There is nothing we can think, say or do, that has not been decreed by God. To the man whose house has just been burnt to the ground there is only one thing to say — Allah katib — God willed it. To the lonely sufferer dying from cancer or tuberculosis, all that can be said is — Allah katib — God willed it. "God misleadeth whom He will and whom He will He guideth" — so says the Koran. Evil is just one of God's many gifts, one of the gifts of a God who is called the "All-merciful," but has ninety-eight other names as well. When God chooses to send evil, none can withstand Him. It is decreed in heaven. Fatalism rules at every level. Real hope is unknown. Such forbidding fatalism is not unknown elsewhere. Bertrand Russell emphasizes the fact that the evolutionary principle supplies no basis whatever for optimism over man or his future destiny. And Thomas Hardy epitomizes humanistic fatalism when he writes of his heroine: "The President of the immortals had finished his sport with Tess." In such a faith Christ has no part.

The Bible rejects any views that suggest the only answer to the problem of pain is the forgetfulness of self-indulgence. It rejects also and in absolute terms any suggestion that evil is a hangover from an animal past and that all we need is a few more billion years to work out the best and let the ape and tiger die. Evil in biblical terms is "exceeding evil." It is an offence to God and an intrusion in His creation. If uncorrected and undetected, it will prove to be man's destruction. Evil is faced in all its forms on every page of the Bible. The story of man has scarcely begun when we are introduced to the Tree of the Knowledge of Good and Evil — and then to the whole plan of divine redemption from evil. Our pressing on for an answer must follow the Bible's leading.

Evil in the light of Scripture — this urgent question has preoccupied Christian theology from the early fathers to the present day. Augustine deals exhaustively with the theme and the Reformers, with their passionate adherence to Scripture as the normative source of Christian truth, were equally involved in the grand debate. Our own twentieth century has contributed greatly — witness Karl Barth's extended writings on the problem of evil in his massive work on *Church Dogmatics*. This is inevitable. For the Bible deals with this subject from the very beginning. We have scarcely begun to read the opening pages of the Bible before we find ourselves participants and not mere spectators in the presentation of the origin and nature of evil. "Out of the ground," writes the Bible's first historian, "made the Lord God to grow every tree that is pleasant to the sight, and good for food; the tree of life also in the midst of the garden, and the tree of the knowledge of good and evil."[1] This is the first mention of "evil" in the Bible. It is not yet an actuality in man's history. It is here only in a potential sense. Ten times already we have read the word "good." God "saw that it was good" — that is one of the recurring phrases of the opening page of the Bible. Now we meet with something else — "the tree of the knowledge of good and evil." It grows at the heart of all this good creation; and further on in the story of chapter two we read, "Of every tree of the garden thou mayest freely eat: but of the tree of the knowledge of good and evil, thou shalt not eat of it: for in the day that thou eatest thereof thou shalt surely die."[2]

We may call this chapter philosophy, or poetry, or prophecy. It is all of these. It is at the same time truth. It is a factual statement of history. The Holy Spirit undoubtedly uses symbols here, but they are symbols of reality — seals of truth. The last two pages of the Bible use symbols to express what otherwise would be inexpressible. The language of the book of Revelation is code language, though the intent is clear and the truth of the overthrow of evil and the triumph of God is unmistakable. Likewise in these opening chapters of the Bible, the same Holy Spirit employs "symbols," that is, what we assume are the best possible media of communicating truth to every man of every nation to the end of time. C. S. Lewis, in referring to the records of Genesis, chapters two and three, makes this pertinent comment: "I assume that the Holy Spirit would not have allowed the story of the tree of the knowledge of good and evil to grow up in the Church and win the assent of great doctors unless it was also true and useful as far as it went." It is in the light of Scripture that Scripture interprets itself. The entire Pauline structure of theology would be meaningless without the Genesis truth. And it is as a revelation of truth that we regard these words of Scrip-

[1]Gen. 2:9.   [2]Gen. 2:16, 17.

ture: "Of the tree of the knowledge of good and evil, thou shalt not eat of it: for in the day that thou eatest thereof thou shalt surely die."

This is where the Bible starts, in teaching about the nature of evil, its powers of destruction, as well as its origin. Here we must start therefore if we want to discover the biblical answer to this profound mystery. Let me repeat something I have already said, namely, that the Genesis narrative is in all probability pictorial — but that does not mean that it is not real. For such a universal audience as is going to hear the truth of the fall of man, God clearly devised a method of presenting truth which could be at the same time symbolical yet historical, pictorial yet real, dramatically simplified yet psychologically more profound than the mind of any generation has been able to plumb. There is no more searching analysis of the essence of sin in all literature than is given in the opening verses of the third chapter of Genesis. Sin evolves in doubt of God, in disbelief in His love, in distrust of His word; and this is followed by illicit desire, first of the flesh ("the fruit was good for food"), next of the eyes ("it was pleasant to behold"), and next of self-glory ("it was a fruit to be desired to make one wise"). All this inner conflict leads to action. Desire moves upon the will, the will consents and the sinful act ensues: "she took of the fruit thereof, and did eat."[3] This is the biblical record of

> Man's first disobedience, and the fruit
> Of that forbidden tree, whose mortal taste
> Brought death into the world, and all our woe,
> With loss of Eden.

It is a record that is miraculous, simple in language, lucid in teaching, and profound in psychological insight. The greatest

[3]Gen. 3:6.

minds of the ages have grappled with it and have found its depths unfathomable and inexhaustible. Yet men of the humblest origin, men and women from the most primitive societies, have read and understood, believed and been blessed. Clearly the record is given — as in all Scripture — "by inspiration of the Spirit of God." Surely none but He could have contracted so much of truth into so brief a span and yet embedded the truth in such immortal prose.

In its presentation of the nature and origin of evil, the Bible makes several distinctive emphases, each of which must be noted carefully.

I

First of all, the Bible affirms that evil does not rightly belong to the nature of man.

That is made absolutely clear. Genesis, chapter one, is the story of creation. "The Spirit of God moved upon the face of the waters"[4]; and by the creative word of God the heavens and the earth were formed. By that word we see uprising the great continental masses, the first flush of vegetation, the dawn of sentient life, the creation of higher forms of animate existence, and all this emergent through ageless aeons of time as we know time, for "one day is with the Lord as a thousand years, and a thousand years as one day."[5] In this matchless story of creation we see the light flashing out of darkness as God said, "Let there be light,"[6] and we sense the ceaseless interplay of volcanic action and electrical discharge, the ocean beds established and their waters filled with animate life. Finally we see man himself, created from the dust yet with his intellectual and moral nature fashioned in the likeness of God. All the colors of God's perfect artistry are seen in their infinite variety, in perfection of order

[4]Gen. 1:2.   [5]2 Pet. 3:8.   [6]Gen. 1:3.

and beauty, and in the unbroken harmony of nature at every point in the process. Over and over again the Holy Spirit tells us that "God saw that it was good" — and at the end we read, "God saw every thing that he had made, and, behold, it was very good."[7] This is the ultimate verdict of God upon the work of His creation. There is no evil in it. All is good.

Into this setting of perfection God places man. He made man "in his own image, in the image of God created he him."[8] God creates man with a moral nature as yet untainted by a single sin. Being made in the image of God, he bears within himself a capacity of choice — a freedom of action which is going to make him vulnerable to temptation to evil. That is the risk God takes when in the sovereignty of omnipotence He gives this gift of His own image to His creature. But in the beginning Adam is without sin. All things are put under his feet — the beasts of the field, the fowls of the air, the fish of the sea. They are all under his dominion and control. And God is with him. God cares for him. God gives a helpmeet to him, for He sees that "it is not good that the man should be alone,"[9] and Eve is created to be at his side. The holy bond of marriage is sanctified by God, and in the blessedness of Eden, Adam and Eve live together, work together, worship together, reign together and rejoice together.

This is the story of the creation of man, and in it there is no place for evil. God and man are truly one. Life and rest and power and joy descend from God to man in the form of divine blessing or gift, and return from man to God in the form of trust, obedience and praise. Every faculty of man is dedicated to the service of God. Every action of man is a token of his filial soul-surrender to his Creator and a prophecy of that ultimate perfection of commitment which the Son of Man our Saviour was to show upon the Cross. In all the record there is no place for evil.

[7]Gen. 1:31.   [8]Gen. 1:27.   [9]Gen. 2:18.

Biblical authority therefore affirms that evil does not belong to the true nature of man.

II

A second affirmation of the Bible is that evil entered our nature — and all the earth around us — from without.

Nothing could be clearer, nothing more emphatic than this. When we move from the end of chapter two of Genesis to the first verse of the third chapter, we move into another realm of experience, which is altogether different. "Now the serpent," we read, "was more subtle than any beast of the field which the Lord God had made."[10] And this serpent approaches Eve. You will recall that the divine law for man had been that of every tree of the garden he should freely eat. Nothing was withheld from him — save one thing. Of the Tree of the Knowledge of Good and Evil he must not partake. This tree, like all the rest, was in the garden that God had created and into which He had put man. Every tree and its fruit was for the possession and enjoyment of man. Across this one tree, however, the divine veto lay. "Thou shalt not eat of it."[11] Adam and Eve know no privation by not partaking of the fruit of this tree. On the contrary, they share the life of God and know His blessing continually. As they respect God's commandment, they are blessed with all spiritual and temporal blessings through every day. The ruling of God, being accepted by them as perfect and good, results in their continued felicity, their unbroken fellowship with heaven, and their freedom from the knowledge of evil.

But the serpent appears. He appears to challenge them on the very point of the divine prohibition. He questions this. He forces them to question its validity. He urges that God has selfish motives of self-interest in denying them the use of this particular

[10]Gen. 3:1.   [11]Gen. 2:17.

tree. "Yea, hath God said this?" "Has He really said that you must not eat of the fruit of every tree of the garden?" Eve's reply is an affirmation of the law of God; and the serpent's further rejoinder is a downright denial of the truth of the word of God. "The serpent said unto the woman, Ye shall not surely die: for God doth know that in the day ye eat thereof, then your eyes shall be opened, and ye shall be as gods, knowing good and evil."[12] Thus the challenge to the authority and veracity of the word of God is spoken – and it comes from a source outside of man.

This is not yet the place nor the time for an examination of the serpent – who he is and whence he comes. In the book of Revelation, however, St. John speaks of "that old serpent, called the Devil, and Satan, which deceiveth the whole world."[13] We shall study this in full detail in Chapter Four, "The Enemy – The Evil One." Here let us note only that from the evidence the Bible supplies, evil entered from without. Through the machinations of the serpent man was tempted; and through yielding to the treachery, the guile and the falsity of the serpent, sin found a lodging in man. Thus we read in Romans 5:12, "By one man sin entered into the world, and death by sin; and so death passed upon all men, for that all have sinned." Dreadful indeed was the fall of that day; and fearful and frightful the entail of the sin that entered the human race under the temptation of the serpent. There and then the spoiling of the species began. But the evil came from without – from outside man himself. The Bible teaches this and nothing else.

III

There follows the third emphasis of the Bible, and it is

[12]Gen. 3:4, 5.   [13]Rev. 12:9.

here that we are shown the real nature of evil — what evil really is. The essence of evil is not to heed, not to trust, not to obey, the proclaimed and heard will of God.

To understand this we must go back to the Tree of the Knowledge of Good and Evil. There may have been nothing exceptional about this tree at all. It may have been similar to many another tree in the garden. It may even have occupied a much less conspicuous place than many of the rest. It was nonetheless unique. It was distinguished by the fact that over it hung the express prohibition of God. The divine veto shadowed this particular tree. "Thou shalt not eat of it." The Tree of the Knowledge of Good and Evil symbolized the perfection of the law of God. At the heart of the garden, God's law ruled. In that law and in obedience to that law, there was peace and joy. But when the door is opened even a little bit to doubt of the rightness and truthfulness of that law, then an entrance is being prepared for evil. True goodness consists in being in the center of the will of God. True evil consists in separation from the will of God and in refusal to return. The will of God is expressed in His word. "The Lord God commanded the man, saying . . . ."[14] God spoke His word. That word revealed His will. And God in speaking to man said, "Thou shalt not eat of this tree." In other words, God gave everything to man — without reserve or constraint — but he would only possess everything by accepting the denial of the one thing that God forbade.

This is what is being taught here in words that a child can understand. The tree in itself might well be nothing, though on that we dare not dogmatize. What is certain is that God's word is everything. To doubt that word and to disobey God's will is an evil thing. To part company with the word and

[14]Gen. 2:16.

will of God is to walk away from God into the dark. This is what evil is, according to the Word of God. This is how it began. When God gave man the gift of the divine image, He gave to him the essential capacity of moral choice. It never was the intent of God to create a company of robots who would automatically and not of their own choice do the good and refuse the evil. No! The plan of God is clearly set forth as the creation of a race of men who will freely cleave to that which is good and abhor that which is evil. The choice will be a real choice. And it may well be that here we glimpse something of the mystery of the divine plan in allowing evil and sin to enter into creation. God will use this very evil to make His children hate evil even as He Himself does. In saying so, we are anticipating some of our later studies. But this is certain — the essence of sin is distrust of and disobedience to the will of God.

And there is here not only the history of the first fall of man into sin; there is a specific analysis of the surrender of any man — and that means of us all — to the thraldom of sin. Evil is always doubt of the will of God. Surrender to evil always begins in distrust of the Word of God. "Yea, hath God said?"[15] — that is the question that all men face when they consider what goodness and virtue really are. Is the Christian ethic an absolute ethic? Or are there other possibilities to what the Christian faith demands? On the great categorical imperatives of the moral law, the Bible never flinches. The commandments are always clear and incisive. But to every man the temptation comes to doubt and disbelieve that these commandments are really true and that apart from them there is no possibility of blessing. God's Word says that there is only one way of salvation — through the sacrifice of Calvary. To doubt this is to

[15]Gen. 3:1.

walk off into the dark, away from God. The fall in the garden
is multiplied a million-fold and is compounded with every new
sin. Sin is transgression of God's commandment.

IV

The Bible stresses another great fact. Evil has affected the
whole creation.

In verses 16 to 19 of chapter three of Genesis we read:

> I will greatly multiply thy sorrow; in sorrow thou shalt bring
> forth children.
> Cursed is the ground for thy sake; in sorrow shalt thou eat
> of it all the days of thy life.
> Thorns also and thistles shall it bring forth to thee.
> In the sweat of thy face shalt thou eat bread, till thou
> return unto the ground; for out of it wast thou taken: for
> dust thou art, and unto dust shalt thou return.

In some mysterious way physical evil followed moral evil. As
a result of this primal sin of man, the whole creation was,
according to Paul, "made subject to vanity."[16] All creation came
under the influence of evil, of failure, of decay. Not only is
man affected by the sin in Eden; the whole existence in which
we live and are involved has come under the bondage of corruption. There is a correspondence between physical evil and
the moral evil of fallen creatures, be they angels or men;
and this is in accordance with the perfect will of God. That
is surely the meaning of Paul's words when he says that "the
creature was made subject to vanity, not willingly, but by
reason of him [that is, God] who hath subjected the same in
hope."[17] All creation shuddered that day under the impact of
man's primal fall; and all creation has since that day shared
in the blight. Earthquakes, disasters, floods, cataclysms, and

[16]Rom. 8:20.   [17]Rom. 8:20.

the like, flow from this fountainhead. Hence come wars and
strife of every kind. Thorns and thistles and briars abound
across creation and have their *fons et origo* in the fall of man.
Childbirth is anguish — and every new birth retells the conse-
quences of sin. Work retains its God-given dignity; but to
toil there is added a component it was never intended to have
— "in the sweat of thy face shalt thou eat bread."[18] And there
are many kinds of sweat — the sweat of going through motions
of work for the sake of dollars and nothing else, the sweat of
strife between management and men, union strife, the lust for
power that will overleap any obstacle that others may upraise in
order to obtain its ends.

And death also. "Dust thou art, and unto dust shalt thou
return."[19] "Death passed upon all men."[20] Vanity and corruption reach their ultimate in the oblivion of death. No wonder
"the whole creation groaneth and travaileth in pain together
until now."[21] Death is the ultimate denial of a creation which
was established by Him who "hath life in himself." But this
is the entail of sin. For the ending of this state of affairs, all
creation waits, looking expectantly for that day when there
shall be manifested the sons of God, the sons of a new creation, the sons of everlasting life over whom death will have
no power. Till that day dawns, however, sin reigns and the
awesome harvest of sin is shared by all.

V

That, however, is not the final word. God would never
leave us there. The final word is that evil shall not absolutely
rule forever in God's universe.

God preaches the Gospel in Eden. He does so first of all to

[18]Gen. 3:19.   [20]Rom. 5:12.
[19]Gen. 3:19.   [21]Rom. 8:22.

the serpent. "And the Lord God said unto the serpent, Because thou hast done this, thou art cursed above all cattle, and above every beast of the field; upon thy belly shalt thou go, and dust shalt thou eat all the days of thy life: and I will put enmity between thee and the woman, and between thy seed and her seed; it shall bruise thy head, and thou shalt bruise his heel."[22] This declaration of enmity between the serpent and the woman, and between her seed and his seed, is the first message of divine redemption in its opposition to, and in its triumph over, sin. This has been called rightly the Protevangelium — the primal prophecy of Him who will come to destroy him that has the power of death and cast him forever out of the universe of God.

The first preaching of the Gospel was to the serpent, though man overheard the message. And rightly so. For the grand drama of redemption has repercussions and effects beyond the human race. At Calvary, where the serpent "bruised" the Son of God and it seemed as though the powers of evil had triumphed, there the devil was really overthrown. Christ "made a show of him openly, and triumphed."[23] This is the hope that breaks in the very hour of man's fall. Hope speaks, for God speaks. There will be a Deliverer who will come from "the seed of the woman" and He will war continually against the dominion of evil. "He shall not fail nor be discouraged, till he have set judgment in the earth: and the isles shall wait for his law."[24] Thus to Adam, and Eve his helpmeet, God opens the door of hope. From Eden they are banished lest they eat of the Tree of Life and live forever in their sin. But from that moment God is at work. The redemptive operations of sovereign grace have already moved into action. Salvation will come, and it will be complete.

The story of the fall ends, therefore, in a note of unshakable

[22]Gen. 3:14, 15.　　[23]Col. 2:15.　　[24]Is. 42:4.

D

confidence and hope. In that hope — and in the power of that hope — we may even now share. We may enter into life through Him who has overcome the sharpness of death, and even now share the triumph of His resurrection life.

CHAPTER FOUR

THE ENEMY — THE EVIL ONE

To Christ, the forces of evil were intensely real and personal. He accepted Satan as an existent being, an enemy of God, and He addressed the demons whom He cast out, not as delusions of sick minds, but as actual. To Him the fact that the demons were deprived of their baleful power over men was clear proof that the kingdom of heaven, the rule of God, was beginning.

Kenneth Scott Latourette, *A History of Christianity*

Our Lord taught in parables. He used many parables. All of them were original, practical and meaningful. There is not one that is not unusual; many of them are counted among the immortal stories of the world. Some He left to His disciples to work out under the guidance of the Holy Spirit in later days. The first two parables, however, were among the ones which He Himself interpreted to His disciples — the parable of the sower and the seed, and the parable of the tares in the field. He was most explicit. He left nothing to chance. He told them in exact words what the meaning of the parables was. And it is extremely significant that in both these parables He deals with the problem of evil, referring in each of them to "the evil one," and indicating in the most specific terms the kind of work "the wicked one" sets out to perform.

In any study of the problem of evil, the parable of the tares must be most carefully examined. In many ways it is the key parable for the discussion of the nature and origin of evil — and also of the nature and works of "the evil one." The story itself is most simple. Here it is.

> Another parable put he forth unto them, saying, The king-
> dom of heaven is likened unto a man which sowed good seed
> in his field.

> But while men slept, his enemy came and sowed tares among the wheat, and went his way.
>
> But when the blade was sprung up, then appeared the tares also.
>
> So the servants of the householder came and said unto him, Sir, didst not thou sow good seed in thy field? from whence then hath it tares?
>
> He said unto them, An enemy hath done this. The servants said unto him, Wilt thou then that we go and gather them up?
>
> But he said, Nay; lest while ye gather up the tares, ye root up also the wheat with the tares.
>
> Let both grow together until the harvest: and in the time of harvest I will say to the reapers, Gather ye together first the tares, and bind them in bundles to burn them: but gather the wheat into my barn.[1]

There is the record. Tares are sown among the wheat — and by an enemy. And the interpretation is perfectly clear. It is summed up in verses 37-39 of the thirteenth chapter of St. Matthew.

> He answered and said unto them, He that soweth the good seed is the Son of man;
>
> The field is the world; the good seed are the children of the kingdom; but the tares are the children of the wicked one;
>
> The enemy that sowed them is the devil; the harvest is the end of the world; and the reapers are the angels.

Thus very clearly, and very early in His ministry, our Lord gives the most explicit teaching concerning "the evil one"—"the enemy," as He calls him. In the Old Testament, we see much of the work of the evil one; but little is said about his person. But now that the Light of the world is come, the shadows are more intense, and the true nature of the dark powers of the devil stands out more sharply. Bengel in his commentary on Ephesians has this pithy comment on the Christian's spiritual

[1]Matt. 13:24-30.

warfare: "The more plainly any book of scripture treats of
the dispensation and glory of Christ, the more clearly, on the
other hand, does it present the opposite kingdom of darkness."
The same truth is stressed by St. Chrysostom when he says:
"This is the order which we perceive in the economy of God.
After the prophets, the false prophets; after the apostles, the
false apostles; after the Christ, the anti-Christ." This is what
our Lord is doing in the first two parables He taught. He breaks
the silence of the ages, and reveals the true nature of "the
enemy — the evil one," exposing him as one whose being is
totally evil and whose intent is to attack the works of God and
the children of God.

That our Lord recognized the presence, the malignity, the
hostility and the undying enmity of an evil one whom He
called the devil, is unmistakable. In every way that superhuman
guile could devise, the evil one tempted our Lord in the wilderness. The facts of the wilderness temptation must have been
told by our Lord to the disciples at some point in His earthly
ministry — possibly even after His resurrection. "He was a
murderer from the beginning, and abode not in the truth,
because there is no truth in him. When he speaketh a lie, he
speaketh of his own: for he is a liar, and the father of it."[2]
He spoke about "the enemy — the evil one." The language is
awesome; but the meaning is unmistakable. Behind all history
there is a personal force of evil, one of whom it can be said,
"There is no truth in him."[3] He is the enemy of God, the foe
of everything righteous, the opposer of the truth. All this is
included in our Saviour's words when He says of the tares in
the field, "the enemy that sowed them is the devil."[4] Elsewhere
He speaks of him as "a strong man armed,"[5] and warns Peter

[2]John 8:44.   [4]Matt. 13:39.
[3]John 8:44.   [5]Luke 11:21.

that "Satan hath desired to have you, that he might sift you
as wheat."[6] He sent out the disciples on a mission of teaching
and healing and when they returned saying that "even the
devils are subject unto us through thy name," He replied, "I
beheld Satan as lightning fall from heaven."[7]

The apostles continue this teaching in all the epistles. They see
the work of Christ as the annulling of the powers of the devil.
The writer of Hebrews says, "Forasmuch then as the children
are partakers of flesh and blood, he also himself likewise took
part of the same; that through death he might destroy him that
had the power of death, that is, the devil; and deliver them, who
through fear of death were all their lifetime subject to bondage."[8]
St. Paul speaks of him as "the prince of the power of the air,
the spirit that now worketh in the children of disobedience"[9];
but he shows them how to overcome and bids them "put on the
whole armor of God, that ye may be able to stand against the
wiles of the devil."[10] Peter sees him as "a roaring lion, walking
about, seeking whom he may devour" — but immediately adds,
"whom resist steadfast in the faith."[11] John, too, is most specific
in what he says. "The devil sinneth from the beginning. For
this purpose the Son of God was manifested, that he might destroy the works of the devil."[12] With all this the book of Revelation fully agrees, referring to the evil one as "that old serpent,
called the Devil, and Satan, which deceiveth the whole world."[13]
At every point and by every pen he is seen as "the enemy — the
evil one," sowing tares among the wheat and deceiving "if it
were possible, the very elect."[14]

Most frequently in the Scripture he is referred to as "Satan"
or "the devil"; but other descriptive titles are occasionally em-

[6]Luke 22:31.   [9]Eph. 2:2.   [12]1 John 3:8.
[7]Luke 10:17, 18.   [10]Eph. 6:11.   [13]Rev. 12:9.
[8]Heb. 2:14, 15.   [11]1 Pet. 5:8, 9.   [14]Matt. 24:24.

ployed which are most revealing. He is "the tempter."[15] He is called "Beelzebub the prince of the devils."[16] At other times he is portrayed in terms which fallen man himself epitomizes — "sinner,"[17] "deceiver,"[18] "murderer."[19] By whatever name, however, he is known or presented, he is consistently seen as the enemy of God and man. Calvin deals with this subject when he writes of the knowledge of God the Creator and summarizes it in his usual blunt way.

> He opposes the truth of God with falsehoods, he obscures the light with darkness, he entangles men's minds in errors, he stirs up hatred, he kindles contention and combats, everything to the end that he may overturn God's kingdom and plunge man with himself into eternal death. From this it appears that he is in nature depraved, evil and malicious. For there must be a consummate depravity in that disposition which devotes itself to assailing God's glory and man's salvation. This also is what John means in his letter when he writes that the "devil has sinned from the beginning," and indeed he clearly considers him as the architect, author and leader of all malice (*Institutes* 1.14.15).

This is the uniform teaching of the Scriptures as a whole. Behind all history is such an enemy of God and men, resolved to overthrow the good and committed to the tempting and the testing of the godly. Our Lord authenticates this teaching and, consequently, there are only three possible alternatives. One is that He Himself was the victim of the gross superstition of His age. The second is that, although He knew better, He nonetheless accommodated Himself to the gross superstition of His age. The third is that, in teaching as He did, He taught the truth. It is this third conclusion which alone vindicates His sincerity, His omniscience and His infallibility. If He is wrong on His teaching about the devil, then He could be wrong on anything else. He

[15]Matt. 4:5; 1 Thess. 3:5.   [17]1 John 3:8.   [19]John 8:44.
[16]Matt. 12:24.   [18]Rev. 12:9.

would thereby not be the Truth. But in His person, His words and His works, He claims to be and manifests Himself as "the way, the truth, and the life."[20] As the Truth, He taught that the doom of Satan was one of the basic objectives of the kingdom of God. "Get thee behind me, Satan,"[21] is His word to any who would hinder Him in His work of redemption. He was born to destroy the works of the devil, and at the Cross, where supremely this was accomplished, He cried, "It is finished."[22] We cannot overemphasize this. It is the unmistakable teaching of our Lord, and it is impossible, therefore, to think about the problem of evil as Christ saw it, without emphasizing the reality of Satan.

Many of course disagree with this position. Classic liberalism, built as it was on idealistic and evolutionary metaphysics, found — and still finds — the subject of Satan and fallen spirits an acute embarrassment. It is especially vexed and perplexed at Christ's acceptance of their existence. But this is something that we have been taught by the Scriptures to expect. Denial of a superhuman ringleader and tempter to evil in the spiritual world is the natural testimony of a culture which is itself deceived by him who "deceiveth the whole world." "The whole world lieth in wickedness,"[23] writes John; and what began at the outset of human history when the enemy of God plunged the human race into guilt by deceiving and seducing its representative, is still continuing. Never is the work of the evil one more clearly manifested than when men doubt his existence and mock at his power. To avoid a doctrine of Satanology is to dodge the reality of human responsibility and deny human hope, since moral evil is then understood as one of the inevitabilities of finite existence. This the Scriptures never do. They see evil against the background of a mighty, invisible, demonic spirit world — but a

20John 14:6.   22John 19:30.
21Matt. 16:23.   231 John 5:19.

world which can be resisted and overcome through grace. The temptation of our Lord in the wilderness is understood as a contest with the devil and the whole biblical evidence leads to only one conclusion, namely, that God sent His Son into the world to combat and to overthrow Satan, "the enemy — the evil one."

The parable of the tares in the field sheds a great deal of light on the subject, and we must give closest attention to the details that are noted here by our Lord in His interpretation. He speaks of Satan as His enemy. It is this one He has come to overthrow. He sees and recognizes the foe. There is no doubt, however, about the ultimate issue. The enemy will be destroyed — not simply by the exercise of omnipotent force but by the use of spiritual weapons. His triumph must be a moral triumph and not one obtained merely by the putting forth of superior strength. Man lost the battle in the Garden of Eden; but now the second Adam confronts the foe. Satan attacks the "seed of the woman" promised in the Garden of Eden so long ago. This time there will be no victory for evil. But let us note the emphases of our Lord in the parable.

I

First of all, we must note the form of address and the title which He gives to Satan. He is "the enemy — the evil one."

From whence does he come? Our Lord says nothing on this subject. The Scriptures as a whole are very reticent. On this fact Calvin comments (*Institutes* 1.14.16):

> Some persons grumble that scripture does not in numerous passages set forth systematically and in detail that fall of devils, its cause, manner, time and character. But because this has nothing to do with us, it was better not to say anything, or at least to touch upon it lightly, because it did not befit the Holy Spirit to feed our curiosity with empty histories to no effect.

There are, however, certain points at which the Scriptures do touch lightly on this subject and we must note them. Peter speaks of fallen angels: "For if God spared not the angels that sinned, but cast them down to hell, and delivered them into chains of darkness, to be reserved unto judgment. . . ."[24] Jude also at verse six of his epistle writes: "And the angels which kept not their first estate, but left their own habitation, he hath reserved in everlasting chains under darkness unto the judgment of the great day." From these two passages it is clear that there was "a first estate" of angels who subsequently fell. They "left their own habitation." By degeneration they fell themselves and were then made the instruments of ruin and fall for others.

There may well be good reasons for the reticence of Scripture on the fall of the angels. God is order and cosmos. But the *diabolos* is the very personification of destruction and confusion, the direct opposite of order and system and cosmos, and especially contrary to the order of the creation of God. It is impossible to make the chaotic world of evil spirits orderly. To attempt to do so is to minimize the exceeding evil of evil. Here may well be the reason for the silence of Scripture on this whole matter. Yet this much is clear. In the beginning there was "a first estate" of the devil — "the enemy — the evil one." This he left. "He left his own habitation."

Is any clue given as to the reason why? There are two passages from the prophets which are extremely suggestive in this area where perforce we see as in a glass darkly. It is a well-known fact of biblical prophecy that oftentimes there is a double fulfilment — an immediate and an ultimate. It is also a recognized feature of much prophetic insight that these men of God saw beyond the earthly dominion of evil to the spirit that inspired it, and indeed to the very heart of evil itself. With this in mind, the

[24]2 Pet. 2:4.

passages in Isaiah 14 and Ezekiel 28 should be read. Both of them obviously refer to earthly monarchs — Isaiah to the king of Babylon; Ezekiel to the prince of Tyre. At the same time it is hard to believe that the references do not go beyond the merely human plane of existence. "How art thou fallen from heaven, O Lucifer, son of the morning! . . . thou hast said in thine heart, I will ascend into heaven, I will exalt my throne above the stars of God: I will sit also on the mount of the congregation, in the sides of the north."[25] This is how Isaiah sees the overweening pride of the king of Babylon; and is it not in accordance with all that is hinted at in the other Scriptures that the devil too wished to "exalt himself above the stars of God"?

Ezekiel is even more explicit in the detail of his imagery. Here are a few of the references in this striking page of the prophet. "Thou sealest up the sum, full of wisdom, and perfect in beauty. Thou hast been in Eden the garden of God; . . . Thou art the anointed cherub that covereth; . . . thou wast upon the holy mountain of God. . . . Thou wast perfect in thy ways from the day that thou wast created, till unrighteousness was found in thee. . . . Thine heart was lifted up because of thy beauty, thou hast corrupted thy wisdom by reason of thy brightness: therefore I will cast thee as profane out of the mountain of God; I will cast thee to the ground, I will lay thee before kings, that they may behold thee."[26]

This obviously cannot refer only to the prince of Tyre. It could never be said of him that he sealed up the sum of wisdom and beauty and was perfect from the day that he was created. A deeper significance is to be found in these fathomless words; and, since Scripture is its own interpreter, this would appear part of a vision God gave to His servant the prophet of the rise of the kingdom of spiritual evil behind the forces of human

[25] Is. 14:12, 13.   [26] Ez. 28:12-15, 16, 17.

history. Wisdom was corrupted by reason of brightness. Because of his beauty, his heart was lifted up. Thus, in the pregnant and meaningful words of St. Jude, "he left his own habitation." The origin of evil lies veiled within the mystery of finite freedom. "Bartering the lofty dignity of eternity for the inflation of pride," writes Augustine in the *City of God* (12.1), "trading the most assured verity for the slyness of vanity, they became proud, deceived, envious."

Thus before the first of time, Satan left his first estate. In this sense "the devil sinneth from the beginning."[27] For this reason he sows the tares among the wheat. He is "the enemy — the evil one."

II

Our Lord proceeds to speak of *the works* of the evil one. He "sowed tares among the wheat."[28] "The tares are the children of the wicked one. The enemy that sowed them is the devil."[29]

Now it has been frequently noted that there is great similarity between tares and good seed while both are in the blade. They are only distinguishable when the ear is formed, and in this sense they fulfil literally our Lord's words, "By their fruits ye shall know them."[30] We see here, however, how guilefully the enemy counterfeits the works of God. He can clothe himself as an angel of light and make his servants appear likewise while all the time he is camouflaging and counterfeiting the true. This is the work of the enemy. "An enemy hath done this."[31] Evil has entered the field which is the world through the activity of "an enemy," and the tares are "the children of the wicked one" — persons who have allowed the evil emanating from the evil one himself to abide and indwell them. Evil is traced to its ultimate source, to

[27]1 John 3:8.
[28]Matt. 13:25.
[29]Matt. 13:38, 39.
[30]Matt. 7:16.
[31]Matt. 13:28.

the direct and distinctive counterworking of the great spiritual enemy. "The enemy that sowed them is the devil."

By the will of God these tares are allowed to grow. "Wilt thou then that we go and gather them up?"[32] The answer was no. The children of the evil one and the children of the kingdom continue side by side. "Let both grow together until the harvest."[33] God knows what He is doing. Evil is permitted on earth — but it will have an end. The evil one is still suffered to sow his seeds of discord and of doubt, but his days are numbered. He cannot, however, alter his nature and through every generation he strives to undermine the true and to deceive all men. The tares take many forms. "The god of this world hath blinded the minds of them which believe not, lest the light of the glorious gospel of Christ, who is the image of God, should shine unto them."[34] He makes the things of time alluring and seemingly real, while he makes the things of eternity distant and unsubstantial. He tempts and seduces a husband and wife like Ananias and Sapphira and makes them "to lie to the Holy Ghost."[35] This is the work of "the enemy — the evil one." He sows the seeds of strife in the church so that Euodias and Syntyche no longer have sweet fellowship together.[36] He tempts the Christian and makes him lukewarm.[37] He raises up false prophets who prophesy peace when there is no peace and who set themselves to declare another way of salvation, another gospel.[38] He invents new devices and cults in every generation and leads multitudes to trust in their false teachings. He deceives nations, brainwashing them and demon possessing them. Always he tempts to disbelief in the Word of God.

By divine permission he is allowed to test God's people. In doing so he is trying to sow tares in the field — *but he need not*

---

[32]Matt. 13:28.   [35]Acts 5:3.   [38]Gal. 1:8, 9.
[33]Matt. 13:30.   [36]Phil. 4:2.
[34]2 Cor. 4:4.   [37]Rev. 3:15.

be successful. Job is tested — but he emerges triumphant through grace divine. Paul is tested. There is given to him "a thorn in the flesh, a messenger of Satan to buffet me,"[39] but he is not cast down, for God said, "My grace is sufficient for thee: for my strength is made perfect in weakness."[40] Daniel was tested as he prayed; but he prayed through to victory.[41] All the saints were tested, and sometimes they fell before the assault of the enemy; but over and over again this is the shout that is heard in their hearts: "Triumph thou not over me, rejoice not against me, O mine enemy: when I fall, I shall arise; when I sit in darkness, the Lord will be a light to me."[42] The works of the evil one are manifold; but for those who seek Him there is always a way of escape.

Every work of God, however, will be counterfeited by the enemy. Behind every work of God there may be seen the "evil one" snatching away the good seed which has been sown in men's hearts and supplanting it with tares. Against such works of the devil it is our duty to watch and pray — and thus enter not into temptation.

III

The third great emphasis of our Lord in the parable of the tares has already been hinted at, but it must be stressed most particularly. There will be an end to the work of "the enemy — the evil one."

> Let both grow together until the harvest: and in the time of harvest I will say to the reapers, Gather ye together first the tares, and bind them in bundles to burn them: but gather the wheat into my barn.

[39]2 Cor. 12:7.   [41]Dan. 10:1-14.
[40]2 Cor. 12:9.   [42]Micah 7:8.

A harvest day is coming. That is what our Saviour says. And He is most explicit as He interprets the parable.

> As therefore the tares are gathered and burned in the fire; so shall it be in the end of this world.
> The Son of man shall send forth his angels, and they shall gather out of his kingdom all things that offend, and them which do iniquity;
> And shall cast them into a furnace of fire: there shall be wailing and gnashing of teeth.[43]

Elsewhere He speaks of this same denouement of evil.

> Depart from me, ye cursed, into everlasting fire, prepared for the devil and his angels.[44]

There will be an end to the power of "the enemy — the evil one." Today he goes about as a roaring lion; but he knows that his time is short. Time will end and the harvest days will come. All things that offend and that do iniquity will be cast out and Satan himself will be cast into what the Bible calls "a furnace of fire." This will be because God is sovereign. "The mystery of iniquity doth already work," writes Paul; "only he who now letteth will let, until he be taken out of the way."[45] Phillips' translation of this passage is most illuminating: "I used to talk about a 're-straining power' which would operate until the time should come for the emergence of [the lawless] man. Evil is already insidiously at work, but its activities are restricted until what I have called the 'restraining power' is removed. When that happens, the lawless man will be plainly seen — though the truth of the Lord Jesus spells his doom, and the radiance of the coming of the Lord Jesus will be his utter destruction." Yes, there will be an end to the "sowing of the tares." There will be an end to the dominion of the evil one. Christian eschatology is full of the brightest hope. The old serpent, the devil, which de-

---

[43]Matt. 13:30, 40-42.   [44]Matt. 25:41.   [45]2 Thess. 2:7.

E

ceiveth the whole world, will be cast down. This is the confidence of the Scriptures. It is a confidence bred and sustained
by the Holy Spirit.

Meantime, we must be on our guard, as we have already said.
We must recognize the malign forces behind our history and,
all too easily and often, behind and in individuals as well. We
dare not underestimate the power of "the enemy – the evil one."
Jude tells us that "Michael the archangel, when contending with
the devil he disputed about the body of Moses, [and] durst not
bring against him a railing accusation, but said, The Lord rebuke
thee."[46] He is powerful; but he is not all-powerful. Our greatest
need as members of the kingdom of our Lord Jesus Christ is for
spiritual discernment so that, like the early Church, we shall be
"able to stand against the wiles of the devil."[47] We need also the
apostolic ability which could take "the shield of faith . . . [and]
be able to quench all the fiery darts of the wicked one."[48] This
was one of the great distinctions of the early Christians. They
were able to pierce through the mere appearance of things and
resist the insidiousness of the foe. They had eyes that were
anointed with grace, and thus they could discriminate between
the profane and the holy. And this watchfulness and spiritual
insight were the gift and the equipping of the Holy Ghost. Every
spark of infernal suggestion, every tendency to biased criticism,
every trend away from the light – these were recognized for what
they were, instruments of the enemy of souls, tools of the devil.
For such spiritual enlightenment and power we must pray. The
devil will take every means and employ every medium to work
towards his ends. He will get into a pulpit, even into a theological
chair, and pretend to teach Christianity, when in actual fact he
is corrupting it. Against all this we must be on our guard, be

[46]Jude 9.   [47]Eph. 6:11.   [48]Eph. 6:16.

sober, be vigilant. We must continually "watch and pray, that [we] enter not into temptation."[49]

The realization that Satan's doom is sealed by God should greatly hearten and encourage us. He is a defeated foe. The victory was won at Calvary. Even as when the troops of the Western world landed on the beaches of France on D-Day, gaining their foothold on the continent of Europe, and Hitler knew that for him the end was near and therefore increased the fury and venom of his folly; so the evil one knows that at the Cross the decisive victory was fought and won by the Son of God. Therefore he strives with even greater might to deceive the unwary and to tempt us all to sin, using every stratagem and glosses innumerable. But the end is sure. The reaping day is coming when the Son of Man shall send forth His angels to gather out all that offends. That day we may even now possess in faith; and doing so, may be victorious over the evil one.

IV

We reach the last point which our Lord stresses in the parable of the tares. He teaches that even in the days of "the enemy — the evil one," the righteous may grow in grace.

> Then shall the righteous shine forth as the sun in the kingdom of their Father. Who hath ears to hear, let him hear.[50]

This is the miracle of sovereign grace. The saints persevere to the end. The secret of the perseverance of the saints is of course the perseverance of their Lord with them and in them. He will not let them go. "He will not suffer thy foot to be moved."[51] He preserves them and keeps them and never suffers them to be tempted above what they are able to endure. It may be that He will suffer "the enemy — the evil one" to test and to try and

49Matt. 26:41.   50Matt. 13:43.   51Ps. 121:3.

sometimes in very severe ways. He may allow Satan to buffet us as St. Paul was buffeted by the thorn in the flesh. Yet through it all His grace will be sufficient and by His great mercy we shall be kept from falling.

The righteous know that all their righteousness comes from their Lord. Therefore they trust in Him. His is the voice that is obeyed. "Resist the devil, and he will flee from you."[52] "Neither give place to the devil."[53] "Put on the whole armor of God, that ye may be able to stand against the wiles of the devil."[54] The "good seed," who are "the children of the kingdom," hear their Master's voice and love to obey. In Him they are safe, saved with an everlasting salvation, so that through Him the seed of the saving Word may be scattered in their generation. Thus they grow in grace and righteousness from day to day. This is the righteous nation which keepeth the peace and which at the last shall find an abundant entrance into the kingdom of their Father on high. This is God's people, a holy people, a sanctified, fearless band, alert, courageous, willing in the day of God's power. The evil one can touch them not as they abide in Christ. And all this is the miracle of grace. In the midst of a fallen, sinful world, the children of the kingdom abide in Christ and conquer in the fight. They overcome Satan by the blood of the Lamb and the word of their testimony. They are indeed more than conquerors through Him that loved them — and loves them still.

---

[52]James 4:7.   [53]Eph. 4:27.   [54]Eph. 6:11.

CHAPTER FIVE

SUFFERING — GOOD OR EVIL?

Cold in the earth — and fifteen wild Decembers
From these brown hills have melted into Spring;
Faithful, indeed, is the spirit that remembers
After such years of change and suffering.

Emily Bronte, *Remembrance*

It is the first condition of our initiation into the secret
society of the Friends of God, that we take our place with
Him before the judgment seat of the world; and are with
Him mocked, patronized and misunderstood by the world's
religion, the world's culture, the world's power — all the
artificial contrivances that it sets up as standards by which
to condemn reality. In the very moment in which we declare
that it cannot give us that intangible kingdom to which we
aspire, we alienate its sympathy, insult its common sense.
Then ignorance, idleness and cowardice condemn us at
their ease, as they once condemned the First and only Fair.

John Cordelier in *The Path of Eternal Wisdom*

To STUDY THE PROBLEM of evil is to be confronted with the fact of suffering. "If suffering is, can God be?" That is a question which has been asked from time immemorial. "If God is good and also omnipotent, then why does He permit suffering in His creation?" This is how men reason. Either there is no spirit behind all things, or else a spirit which is quite heedless and indifferent to good and evil, or worse still, an evil spirit.

Late or soon almost all men meet with suffering. It takes many forms. There is the suffering caused by physical pain, varying in degree but always potentially overwhelming. Pain may be a purely physical sensation. It may be a dull pain or a sharp pain. A large medical and physiological literature is available on the subject of pain, but the writers agree that it is impossible to define pain. More than a hundred years ago the theory was advanced that pain was the effect of an overloading of sensory nerves stimulated by excessive application of heat or cold or noise or pressure of any kind. Few hold this theory today. Evidence has accumulated to show that there are specific pain-receptor nerves, quite separate from those that transmit heat or touch or cold. Much research is at present taking place on what are called "free nerve endings," which are the finest terminal branch roots from a nerve cell whose body lies close to the spinal cord; the present indications of this research are that these nerve endings can communicate both pain and other sensations. We are fearfully and wonderfully made and within our nerve structure there is a machinery that can in a moment strike a man down or over a long period of time can continue to cripple and incapacitate him from normal activity. Instinctively, we avoid pain. Except in abnormal psychic states, pain is universally regarded as an enemy to be avoided at all costs.

Pain causes suffering if it passes a certain point. But there are many forms of suffering which do not radiate from physical pain. Fear and anxiety can create great suffering. Humiliation, a sense of injustice, the loss in death of a loved one, remorse, marriage breakdown, frustration and personal estrangement can cause the acutest suffering. Emotional suffering of this kind can be every bit as severe as that caused by physical pain. The lives of countless people are darkened through the bitterness of failure in ambition or in business, made heavy-laden by the torment of uncertainty, emptiness and despair. Roaming the streets of our great cities are many who have yielded to alcoholism, drug addiction, divorce and crime, not because of the threat of starvation but because of the moral paralysis of the meaninglessness of life as a whole. Suffering is a very complex thing, embracing the mind, the emotions and the total spirit of man. Deep depression is a dread reality for hosts of men and women. Selfishness, greed, lust, cruelty and the resolve for revenge can bring on others a terrifying weight of pain. Add to this the suffering of the orphan and the refugee, the hungry hopelessness of war-torn lands, the unbelievable yet all-too-true obscenities of Belsen and Dachau, the crude lusts and darkness of ancient races reaching back into primeval time, and we have a composite picture of a universe of suffering that is very stark, very frightening and very devilish.

Can suffering be regarded in any light as good? Or is it altogether evil? The question cannot be bypassed. What has the Bible to say to this?

The Scriptures have a great deal to say concerning suffering. For one thing, they are very definite in saying, as we have already noted, that suffering entered the human race after sin entered it. Thorns and briars affect the creation of God after the fall of man, and these thorns and briars are of many kinds. Sorrow and suffering flow from sin; and death, the ultimate of human evil, is the wages of sin. All the woes of a suffering humanity are scanned and probed and enlightened by the Scriptures. Indeed, it can truly be said that no book has ever mirrored the intensity of human suffering, its breadth and universality, its varied forms, and its bewildering perplexities, as the Bible does. Yet through it all, there is no hopelessness nor despair in the biblical analysis of the human situation. On the contrary, a vein of sacred joy runs through all the pages of revelation, and the ultimate issue prophesied by the Scriptures is a new creation, with new heavens and new earth, from which suffering and pain are banished forever. Even while suffering is met on earth, there are also the wonderful promises of God, hope-creating and life-begetting. Realism we meet on every page of the Bible; but pessimism never. "All things work together for good to them that love God."[1] That is God's promise, and it is absolute. In the valley of the shadow of death, amidst the whirlwind and the flame, when disease strikes our mortal body and it weakens towards the grave, through the havoc of earthquake, flood and disaster, His promise abides: "When thou passest through the waters, I will be with thee; and through the rivers, they shall not overflow thee."[2] This is what God covenants to do. He will never leave, will never forsake, His own.

[1] Rom. 8:28.   [2] Is. 43:2.

And it is surely significant that the men of faith do not demand of God that He justify His ways to them. Another factor has come into play in their lives. They are men with minds and so they think things through rationally. Inevitably they ask questions about suffering. They wrestle with the problem which such an intrusion in creation makes urgent for them. But they do not blame God. They do not angrily demand that God explain or defend His conduct. The new factor of faith has taken over in their lives, and this proves stronger than mere intellect. God is real to them — even in the valley of suffering. So we hear them singing even there. The valley of Baca becomes a well. The desert wastes are overblown by the melodies of a sublime confidence in God. Here is Habakkuk. He faces grim and stark days. But what does he say? Listen to him: his words are counted among the noblest ever uttered by mortal man.

> Although the fig tree shall not blossom, neither shall fruit be in the vines; the labor of the olive shall fail, and the fields shall yield no meat; the flock shall be cut off from the fold, and there shall be no herd in the stalls:
> Yet I will rejoice in the Lord, I will joy in the God of my salvation.[3]

The same is true of Job. Inevitably he is perplexed at his suffering. There is no rational category into which he can fit it. The arguments of his friends only depress him more. His wife urges him to curse God and die. But, though for a time it seems as though he is going to go under, he doesn't. "Though he slay me, yet will I trust in him."[4] That is his answer. He cannot account for his sufferings on any rational basis. Yet he is prepared in faith to accept the possibility that God is in them and has some purpose of love behind them all. We meet a similar confidence in Jeremiah. He is known to us as the weeping prophet — and

[3]Hab. 3:17, 18.   [4]Job 13:15.

rightly so, for few suffered as he. He tells of some of his suffering:

> I am the man that hath seen affliction by the rod of his wrath.
> He hath led me, and brought me into darkness, but not into light.
> Surely against me is he turned; he turneth his hand against me all the day.

Yes! God has afflicted him very sorely. But what follows?

> It is of the Lord's mercies that we are not consumed, because his compassions fail not.
> They are new every morning; great is thy faithfulness.[5]

This is the confidence of the saints. God is their confidence. He is their strength.

And Peter, when he writes his first letter to the Church at large, gives us one of the great classic passages on this undying theme.

> Beloved, think it not strange concerning the fiery trial which is to try you, as though some strange thing happened unto you.
> But rejoice, inasmuch as ye are partakers of Christ's sufferings; that, when his glory shall be revealed, ye may be glad also with exceeding joy.[6]

Here is St. Peter's answer to the question: "Suffering — good or evil?" With typical apostolic optimism he says that the sufferings of the Christian can become a wonderful instrument of grace. The sufferings may be sharp and fiery but they are intended to test the believer and not to ruin him. They are of the same quality as were his Lord's sufferings and will lead to the same glory. Mercy is mingled with judgment. The Christian therefore will trust in the Lord and recognize the mercy that is behind such chastisement. The greatest wonder is that even when

[5]Lam. 3:1-3, 22, 23.   [6]1 Pet. 4:12, 13.

there seems no clue to the maze of weakness and of woe, the songs of faith are still heard clearly. "All things work together for good to them that love God."[7] "And I am persuaded, that neither death, nor life, nor angels, nor principalities, nor powers, nor things present, nor things to come, nor height, nor depth, nor any other creature, shall be able to separate us from the love of God, which is in Christ Jesus our Lord."[8]

Now it is this same emphasis which Peter makes in his first letter to the Church. He knows full well the suffering that many of his fellow Christians are enduring and the still heavier trials that may lie ahead; but he writes without reserve to them and encourages them to "arm themselves with the mind of Christ" and to face the trial without fear. His vital stresses are worth our close attention.

I

First of all, St. Peter reminds the believers that Christ Himself suffered; and he tells them that they are "partakers of Christ's sufferings" in what they now endure. "Forasmuch then as Christ hath suffered for us in the flesh, arm yourselves likewise with the same mind."[9] "Rejoice, inasmuch as ye are partakers of Christ's sufferings."[10] The remembrance of their Master's sufferings will sanctify and temper their suffering and pain.

The Christian answer to the problem of suffering must come face to face with this supreme fact. Apart from it, there is really no answer. But the Scriptures are very emphatic on this. The prophets saw Him thus: "a man of sorrows, and acquainted with grief."[11] The Gospels present Him as One who "himself took our infirmities, and bare our sicknesses."[12] The apostles declare that He "made himself of no reputation, and took upon him the

[7]Rom. 8:28.   [9]1 Pet. 4:1.   [11]Is. 53:3.
[8]Rom. 8:38, 39.   [10]1 Pet. 4:13.   [12]Matt. 8:17.

form of a servant, and was made in the likeness of men: and being found in fashion as a man, he humbled himself, and became obedient unto death, even the death of the cross."[13] And further, "hereunto were ye called: because Christ also suffered for us, leaving us an example, that ye should follow his steps."[14] Even more than this is revealed. The reason for the suffering is detailed. "Though he were a Son, yet learned he obedience by the things which he suffered; and being made perfect, he became the author of eternal salvation unto all them that obey him."[15] It is a noteworthy fact that whenever the example of Christ is presented to us in the Scriptures for our imitation, it is His example in suffering which is cited.

This is highly significant. Our Lord undoubtedly possessed the disposition of obedience from the beginning of His days on earth. It was, however, in the school of suffering that He learned the practice of obedience. Through a long curriculum of trial and suffering, He learned obedience. Exemption from suffering would have meant exemption from leadership. "It became him, for whom are all things, and by whom are all things, in bringing many sons unto glory, to make the captain of their salvation perfect through suffering."[16] Suffering was carved on every step that Jesus took. For this reason, "in that he himself hath suffered being tempted, he is able to succor them that are tempted."[17]

If we are to answer the question "Suffering — good or evil?", we must start here. At the heart of history is Jesus Christ. He was made perfect through suffering. He freely submitted Himself to the agony and the ignominy of the Cross, and He suffered there for all men. In doing so, He drained the cup of suffering to the dregs. Suffering became Him. God used suffering

13Phil. 2:7, 8. 15Heb. 5:8, 9. 17Heb. 2:18.
141 Pet. 2:21. 16Heb. 2:10.

to prepare Him for the ultimate sacrifice. He became incarnate
that He might learn obedience. He bore the divine will as a yoke
instead of wielding it as a sceptre. This is the credo of the
Christian. Christ Himself has tasted suffering at the deepest
depths. Therefore He understands. Therefore He can succour
the sufferer and the tried.

II

Another point that St. Peter stresses is that suffering for the
Christian may be "in the will of God." Here are his words: "If
any man suffer as a Christian, let him not be ashamed; but let
him glorify God on this behalf. . . . Wherefore, let them that
suffer according to the will of God commit the keeping of their
souls to him in well-doing, as unto a faithful Creator."[18]

Suffering — in the will of God? In one sense, Yes. Peter has
already spoken about "the fiery trial that is to try them" and
now he speaks about this trial being "in the will of God."
We have seen before that suffering is an intrusion in God's
creation. It was never intended to be there at all. But sin
entered, and with sin came suffering and conflict, pain and
drudgery, corruption and death. In this sense suffering was never
in the will of God. Yet, here is Peter speaking about the saints
of God "suffering as Christians and suffering according to the
will of God." Obviously, then, God can use suffering as an
instrument of His will and for His glory. Even as our Lord
was perfected through suffering, so God can perfect that which
concerns His children even through the fiery furnace of deep
affliction.

Job knew this. He suffered long. He passed through the
dark valley of humiliation, affliction, loss of property, misunder-
standing, loneliness, bereavement, and a deep, deep sense of

[18] 1 Pet. 4:16, 19.

forsakenness by God. He could not see the reason why. Not till the end of the story is there any clue given to Job as to why all he suffered was permitted by God. But this he learned — his suffering was God-ordained, and used of God to bless his own spirit with a deeper understanding of God than he had ever known before. "I have heard of thee by the hearing of the ear; but now mine eye seeth thee: wherefore I abhor myself, and repent in dust and ashes."[19] From the beginning of his travail, however, *we* have known things that Job did not know. We have known that Satan was involved. We have been told that Satan had accused Job before God, saying, "Doth Job fear God for nought?"[20]; and God had said to the evil one, "Behold, all that he hath is in thy power; only upon himself put not forth thine hand. So Satan went forth from the presence of the Lord."[21] The evil one is always the accuser of the people of God. In Job's case, he argued that Job was doing right because of the profit he was deriving from it. To this, God answered: "All right, go ahead; test him as you will, only spare his life." And Satan did just that. He went out to exercise on Job all that a malign and evil imagination could conjure up. He did so by divine permission. Thus Job suffered — but it was "in the will of God."

The same is true of St. Paul. To him were given some very special blessings. He was at one time caught up into Paradise and heard things unspeakable, things which it is not lawful for a man to utter. Then something different happened. Here are his words. "Lest I should be exalted above measure through the abundance of the revelations, there was given to me a thorn in the flesh, the messenger of Satan to buffet me."[22] Strange, is it not? Who would have thought that a man so

19Job 42:5, 6.   21Job 1:12.
20Job 1:9.   222 Cor. 12:7.

signally blessed of God with special revelation and grace should
be allowed to become the target of Satan and to become plagued
with "a thorn in the flesh"? But so it was. He himself could
not understand it. Earnestly he prayed that it might be removed. "For this thing I besought the Lord thrice, that it might
depart from me."[23] God answered his prayer in the negative.
"He said unto me, My grace is sufficient for thee: for my strength
is made perfect in weakness."[24] The thorn was not taken away.
The suffering continued — we do not know what form it took
— but it was not removed. Grace, however, was given. In the
will of God, the suffering was used to humble, to chasten, to
guide, to sanctify this mighty servant of the Lord, and to give
blessing through him. Through suffering God's child was kept
low at his Master's feet.

This we still affirm. Suffering can be "in the will of God."
There are those of course who deny this and blame the sufferer
for lack of faith in not accepting or claiming God's healing,
God's total deliverance from all suffering. How often, however,
are the saints of the Bible presented to us in the valley of affliction! How often is their cry heard "out of the depths"! Grace
holds them there and trains them there. They reach the heavenly
city at length, but they come bloodstained and battle-scarred.
It is through fire and flood that they are safely brought into
the wealthy places of God's heritage. This for them was the
will of God. In that perfect will, which planned that suffering
should have its part, they were themselves made perfect.

Neither God's mercies nor His methods change. Grace still
reigns. God knows what He is doing. With mercy and with
judgment He weaves for us the pattern of life's way. Some
He still entrusts with suffering. Such suffering will never be
easy, but no lesson is without its value when God is the teacher.

[23] 2 Cor. 12:8.   [24] 2 Cor. 12:9.

He has His perfect plan for all His children both for the
present and the future life; and we may be certain that no
lesson, however seemingly trivial or important, painful or pleasant, will be purposeless. Daily we must learn to trust Him
fully. Daily we must cast all our care upon Him. Daily, too,
we must follow through the counsel which St. Peter gives us
in this great message on suffering, "Let them that suffer according to the will of God commit the keeping of their souls
to him in well-doing, as unto a faithful Creator."[25]

III

Yet another note is sounded by the apostle. It is a note which
rises from the deeps of mystery; but it is heard again and again
in the New Testament, and we must be attentive to it here.
Suffering can be a "sharing in" and a "filling up" of our
Saviour's sufferings. "Ye are partakers of Christ's sufferings"
— that is how Peter phrases it here.[26] In suffering we share in
the sufferings of our Lord.

For this reason, St. Paul longed to know "the fellowship of
his sufferings, being made conformable unto his death."[27] So
also he could say, "As the sufferings of Christ abound in us,
so our consolation also aboundeth by Christ."[28] To the Colossian
church he could write, "I now rejoice in my sufferings for you,
and fill up that which is behind of the afflictions of Christ in
my flesh for his body's sake, which is the church."[29] Now this,
as we have already said, is a great mystery. We cannot suggest
that by our suffering we add in any way to the perfection of
our Saviour's work upon the Cross. The salvation He won
for all men is a perfect salvation, the result of a perfected work.
Yet in some divine way, the sufferings of the children of God

25 1 Pet. 4:19.   27 Phil. 3:10.   29 Col. 1:24.
26 1 Pet. 4:13.   28 2 Cor. 1:5.

F

can "complete" or "fill up" the sufferings of Christ. Suffering truly accepted as a trust from God will demonstrate to Satan and his angels the continuing power of the grace of God. It will also manifest to our generation that God is faithful to His promise to support and sustain us, and never to allow us to be tempted beyond our capacity to endure. To suffer in the will of God and to accept it as from His hand in the assurance that it will yet bring forth a harvest of glory is to live in the power of Christ's resurrection, and in that way too to demonstrate that He is in all things the Victor. Writing of this Dean Alford nobly says:

> The tribulations of Christ's Body are Christ's tribulations. Whatever the whole church has to suffer, even to the end, she suffers for her perfection in holiness and her completion in Him; and the tribulations of Christ will not be complete till the last pang shall have passed, and the last tear has been shed. Every suffering saint of God in every age and position is in fact filling up, in his place and degree, the affliction of Christ. This he does in his own mortal body but it is for the church's sake, for the Body of Christ.

Here again we see how God will use suffering to bring good to His own. To shrink from suffering is to shrink from what is a requisite part of our education both for earth and heaven. We may indeed drink of the cup from which our Saviour drank and be baptized with the baptism that He was baptized with.[30] He left the glory of heaven in order that He might lift His servants to a share in that glory. Can we rightly be called His soldiers if we are not following in His steps, bearing His reproach, suffering with Him outside the gate? Can we really expect to be lifted into the companionship of His glory if we are not numbered among those who know "the fellowship of his sufferings"? Can we truly witness to His faithfulness

[30]Mark 10:39.

and saving power if we have not tested these in the fires of affliction and pain?

IV

All has not yet been said. St. Peter reminds us that for the Christian all the sufferings of time must be set against the background of the glory of the revelation of Jesus Christ. "Rejoice, inasmuch as ye are partakers of Christ's sufferings; that, when his glory shall be revealed, ye may be glad also with exceeding joy."[31]

This is the Christian hope. We do not yet see all things put under Christ's feet. Satan is still on the prowl, dangerously near us always. But we see the Saviour and look forward to the crowning day. As he thinks of this, St. Paul says, "I reckon that the sufferings of this present time are not worthy to be compared with the glory which shall be revealed in us."[32] This is the confidence of the saints. For them, whatever their Lord ordains is right. Though sorrow, grief and pain may come, believers know that they are not forsaken and are content to trust and obey their Master's commands. They know that heaven will explain all mysteries, even the mystery of the sufferings that they have borne. They look for their Lord. They watch and wait daily at His gates. They believe that nothing is without meaning, nothing without significance. And until the Lord Himself is revealed in His glory, they take on trust whatever He may send.

> If we could push ajar the gates of life
>   And stand within and all God's workings see,
> We could interpret all this doubt and strife,
>   And for each mystery could find the key.

[31] 1 Pet. 4:13.   [32] Rom. 8:18.

> *But not today! Then be content, poor heart!*
>   *God's plans like lilies pure and white unfold;*
> *We must not tear the close-shut leaves apart,*
>   *Time will reveal the calyxes of gold.*
> *And if through patient toil we reach that land,*
>   *Where tired feet, with sandals loosed, may rest,*
> *Where we shall clearly see and understand —*
>   *I think that we shall say, "God knew the best."*

Against that day we "commit the keeping of [our] souls to him in well doing, as unto a faithful Creator." In the expectation of that day, we "rejoice, inasmuch as [we] are partakers of Christ's sufferings"; and we do so with the assurance that "when his glory shall be revealed, [we] may be glad also with exceeding joy."

CHAPTER SIX

HISTORY — MAN'S CHOICE OF EVIL

Our planet earth, on its journey through infinity, has acquired the intimacy, the fellowship, and the vulnerability of a spaceship. But today the differences and disproportions between various parts of our world community are so great that agreed policies of co-operation run into reefs of hostility and envy. The gaps in power, the gaps in wealth, the gaps in ideology which hold the nations apart also make up the abyss into which mankind can fall to annihilation.
Barbara Ward in Spaceship Earth

Peoples and governments never have learned anything from history, or acted on principles deduced from it.
Friedrich Hegel, Philosophy of History

The kingdoms of this world are become the kingdoms of our Lord, and of his Christ; and he shall reign for ever and ever.
Revelation of St. John 11:15

SOME YEARS BEFORE World War II, Winston Churchill wrote: "Certain it is that while men are gathering power and knowledge with ever-increasing speed, their virtues and their wisdom have not shown any noticeable improvement as the centuries have rolled. Under sufficient stress — starvation, terror, warlike passion or even cold intellectual frenzy, the modern man we know so well will do the most terrible deeds, and his modern woman will back him up."

That may seem a very depressing statement, and no doubt it was intended that it should be so. But it is realistic. It recognizes facts as facts and rejects the kind of facile view of history which sees man growing up into maturity and leaving behind him the crudities and the cruelties of earlier ages. The truth is that we live in a very evil world. Even Gibbon reached the depressing conclusion in his *Decline and Fall of the Roman Empire* that "history is little more than a register of the crimes, follies and misfortunes of mankind." And Dean Inge, with his characteristic, abrupt insight into human situations, had no hesitation in saying that "the devil has frequently captured the

83

organizations which were formed to defeat him, and then used them to his own ends."

The Bible, of course, has its own philosophy of history. All history, it affirms, begins with God, is under God, and will end in the will of God. But the biblical exposure of moral evil in human history is very dark and devastating. Sin is everywhere. According to the Bible, you cannot understand history unless you recognize the ugly reality of demonic evil behind history and the bias of man's heart towards evil from birth to death. When St. Paul wrote to Timothy he said to him, "Evil men and seducers shall wax worse and worse, deceiving, and being deceived,"[1] giving us in a nutshell the history we know and experience, the history of yesterday and of today. "Iniquity shall abound," said our Lord, "[and] the love of many shall wax cold."[2] This is the real story of human history, the story of man's unbroken choice of evil. He taints everything that he touches. He draws the highest things downwards, mixes them with earth and beslimes them with his own cupidity. Near the end of His ministry, our Lord gave a preview of history: the words He uses most frequently are: deception, war, famine, pestilence, earthquake, sorrows, hatred, selfishness, false prophets, iniquity, and the loss of love for God. This is our world. It has always been so. The sins of Nineveh and Tyre yesterday are the sins of Toronto and Tokyo today. Pride makes man as heedless of God in the twentieth century as it has always done. Irresistibly man is drawn to evil; and according to the Bible the only difference between one generation and those preceding it is an acceleration of the speed of degeneracy. Chaos and confusion will be permitted to increase until it has been made utterly clear before men, angels and demons that evil

[1] 2 Tim. 3:13.   [2] Matt. 24:12.

is self-consuming and that no will apart from the will of God can restore order, righteousness and peace to the earth.

This our Lord clearly taught. He describes the world as it will be when He returns and He compares it — not with some of the golden days when Israel sought the Lord — but with the terrible days before the flood when iniquity and the deep, deep rebellion of the human race had reached a climax which demanded judgment. "As the days of Noah were, so shall also the coming of the Son of man be. For as in the days that were before the flood they were eating and drinking, marrying and giving in marriage, until the day that Noah entered into the ark, and knew not until the flood came, and took them all away; so shall also the coming of the Son of man be."[3] And again, "Likewise also as it was in the days of Lot; they did eat, they drank, they bought, they sold, they planted, they builded; but the same day that Lot went out of Sodom it rained fire and brimstone from heaven, and destroyed them all. Even thus shall it be when the Son of man is revealed."[4] In our Lord's analysis of the human heart in every age, pessimism is dominant; and, apart from divine grace, man can do nothing to help himself. All history is a story of man's choosing the evil, of man, the architect of his own ruin. The utter irrationality of human behavior is apparent at every level — among the most primitive peoples such as the bushmen of the Kalahari desert, and in the computerized, technological, sophisticated cities of the peoples of the east or of the west. Sin is the inescapable factor in our history; and if you have difficulty in believing so, remember that, though we have become neighbors in instant communication through the Tel-star and Early Bird satellites, and though we have become neighbors in facets of industrialization and in the patterns of our urbanization, we

[3]Matt. 24:37-39.   [4]Luke 17:28-30.

have also become neighbors in the risk of total destruction. Our Lord said it would be so. The newspaper on our breakfast table is all the confirmation we need of the truth of His analysis of the world of man.

The Bible is the story of man, and from the beginning man has chosen evil. Set in the Garden of Eden, man chose evil rather than good and fell from grace. This is recorded in the third chapter of Genesis, and by the time we reach chapter six we read that "God saw that the wickedness of man was great in the earth, and that every imagination of the thoughts of his heart was only evil continually."[5] Then came the flood and the promise of a new beginning; but by the time we arrive at chapter eleven a people have arisen who are determined to build a tower that will reach to heaven and thus perpetuate their name. God is not in their thoughts. He is the forgotten one. What follows is in the same strain. The men of the cities of the plain are "wicked and sinners before the Lord exceedingly."[6] Sodomy establishes itself in Sodom. The tribes of Canaan become synonyms for abomination and lusts. Egypt oppresses and the Philistines come only to devour. Assyria swoops down like a wolf on the fold while Babylon carries away the inhabitants of Israel and Judah into captivity.

All this the prophets saw and understood. Under the inspiration of the Holy Spirit they were able to see their day in its essence. They listened to its heartbeat and heard the ominous murmurs of impending doom. Amos, with his uncanny ability to read the lessons of history, scanned the nations around and spoke to them about their sins. "The Lord will roar from Zion," he writes, "and utter his voice from Jerusalem; and the habitations of the shepherds shall mourn, and the top of Carmel shall wither."[7] Why? Why this anger and fury of God? Be-

[5]Gen. 6:5.   [6]Gen. 13:13.   [7]Amos 1:2.

cause of the sins of the nations, "For three transgressions of Damascus, and for four, I will not turn away the punishment thereof; because they have threshed Gilead with threshing instruments of iron."[8] But Damascus is not alone. Outrage after outrage is detailed of all the nations encircling Israel — Philistia, Tyre, Edom, Ammon, Moab. Nor do Judah and Israel escape. They, too, have transgressed and done wickedly. And all these nations are summoned to the bar of divine judgment. They are cited before the supreme Judge, "who loveth judgment." The message is clear. God has seen their sin. He has noted their evil ways and does not condone them. In God's sight there is no special kind of morality for politicians or diplomatists. The law of Mount Sinai covers the sins of nations as well as the sins of individuals. National interests provide no cover from the moral law. This is what Amos saw and what he declared to his generation as well as to every subsequent generation. God's justice is not blind. He looks upon the heart and knows what our hearts contain. Therefore "God will roar from Zion, and utter his voice from Jerusalem." For treachery and injustice stalk the streets and righteousness is far removed. This is man's choice. He cleaves to that which is evil, both individually and corporately. In unrighteousness he holds down the good.

Nowhere is this seen more clearly than at Calvary. In the fullness of the times God sent His Son into the world. Incarnate love walked among men but they despised and rejected Him. "Then cried they all again, saying, Not this man, but Barabbas. Now Barabbas was a robber."[9] In all man's history there is nothing more disastrous than this. He chooses a murderer in place of Christ. He condemns the Man of Galilee to the Cross. The same fate awaits His servants. The Church is persecuted by the world, the saints are martyred, the truth is re-

[8]Amos 1:3.   [9]John 18:40.

jected. In the midst of this persecution, John is banished to the isle of Patmos and there, under the inspiration of the Holy Spirit, is given an intense insight into the very heart of all history. He sees one great city — Babylon — and he calls her "the mother of harlots and abominations of the earth."[10] This Babylon is the concentration of everything that entices man from God, the concentration of the luxury, vice and glamor of this world. It is represented as a mighty center of industry, art, commerce, culture and sophistication. Its real heart, however, is godless and its true intent is the seduction of people away from God and into sin. This city is as old as man. It endures through every age, past, present and future. It never changes. The form may vary; but the essence is always the same. The empires of the ancient world are summed up in this one name — Babylon; be it Shinar under Nimrod, the Egyptian Pharaohs, Assyria, New-Babylonia, the Medo-Persian dynasty, the Greco-Macedonian reign, the Roman Empire — all are included and all are the same. They are founded on force and impregnated with vice. Of them all John says, "These have one mind, and shall give their power and strength unto the beast. These shall make war with the Lamb."[11] This is the history of man from the standpoint of heaven. The world in which we live is an arrogant, pleasure-loving, wicked and seductive world which, when the chips are down, will always choose that which is evil and turn away from that which is good.

As we might expect, it is to St. Paul that we are indebted for the most exact and exhaustive analysis of the human situation. In Romans, chapter three, he probes the heart of man and gives this diagnosis, drawn largely from the Psalms:

> *There is none righteous, no, not one:*

[10]Rev. 17:5.   [11]Rev. 17:13, 14.

> *There is none that understandeth,*
> *There is none that seeketh after God.*
> *They are all gone out of the way,*
> *They are together become unprofitable;*
> *There is none that doeth good, no, not one.*
> • *Their throat is an open sepulchre;*
> *With their tongues they have used deceit;*
> *The poison of asps is under their lips:*
> *Whose mouth is full of cursing and bitterness:*
> *Their feet are swift to shed blood;*
> *Destruction and misery are in their ways;*
> *And the way of peace have they not known:*
> *There is no fear of God before their eyes.*[12]

This is the biblical pessimism concerning man stated in its most absolute form. There is a fatal, gravitational pull downwards in man that he is unable to correct. Sin has infected his mind, his emotions, his conscience, his imagination. And sin, when it is finished, brings forth death.

In a recent book, Miss Barbara Ward, a political scientist of world-wide stature and former Editor of the *Economist,* writes of the possibility of nuclear holocaust facing the world through "two or three acts of grandiloquent incineration"; she comments, "How strange it is, that after perhaps a hundred millennia, we should come back to the possibility of retreating once more into caves in order to survive." Strange indeed! Yet this is the order of the day. All the fearful struggles of nations in the past seem insignificant when measured against the darkness of the pall that now overhangs all mankind. At the end of the middle ages Portugal, Spain, Holland, Britain and France sought to establish great commercial empires and they

[12]Rom. 3:10-18.

fought one another each step of the way. When the old Turkish empire crumbled, the Balkans became one of the great "mush areas" of Europe, and Russia and Germany maneuvered into position for the great take-over bid. Two world wars resulted. In the wake of these wars, other world powers emerged to take up the challenge for world hegemony — Russia, China and the United States of America. Cuba and the Congo are glaring illustrations of the conflict that has resulted. But no part of the world is free from the bid of the aggressor. Southeast Asia, the Middle East, Africa and Latin America are the objects of ceaseless barrages of radio and press propaganda. Meantime France, led by the pathological egotism of General de Gaulle, feeds the old passion of total nationhood and demands the appalling prestige symbol of her own nuclear bomb. Vietnam becomes the arena in which conflicting ideologies wage war against each other, and her stoic people become the helpless, hapless victims of jet bombers and flame-throwing tanks. More than 140 billions of dollars are being spent today by world powers in order to guard against the terror of nuclear destruction. Yet all the time, the danger grows greater, and at almost apocalyptic speed the world roars ahead towards destruction.

No area is immune. The Germany of the Reformation, of Luther and of Bach, becomes the Germany of Nietzsche and Hitler. The United States of America, with its great Declaration of Independence stating, *inter alia*, the self-evident truth "that all men are created equal," is torn by racial strife unequalled in her history. India and Pakistan have recently erupted into open conflict over Kashmir and no solution is in sight. The Arab League may be unable to agree among themselves; but with fanatical dedication they are united on the one supreme objective of the ultimate destruction of the nation Israel. One problem may be solved today; but another will raise its head tomorrow. The stuff of deadlock and violence is littered round the world. A divided Korea and a divided Vietnam gave birth to war. What are we to expect from a still divided Germany? The old pan-Slavism is displaced by Communism — but the traditional solutions of annexation, conquest and counter-occupation are still perpetuated. There is no real peace. A sort of security may for a time be found on earth; but it is based on a balance of terror — an appallingly precarious base.

Add to this the labor strife of our times, with the resort to violence during strikes if demands are not granted; the domestic breakdown of our generation and what has been called the "consecutive polygamy" of this century; the financial empires built on pornography. Out of it all there emerges a composite picture which in the most remarkable way tallies with the biblical view of man. There is good reason for the biblical pessimism. We are all brothers — we are all Cains and Abels. Man is a prey to moral degeneracy. His history is a choice of evil rather than of good. He finds his own sins repeated in his children. Try as he may, he cannot escape from the sin that is crushing and destroying his highest efforts. When he would do good, evil is present with him. Sin, which once he considered his choice, is now his master.

If that were all we had to say, despair would hold the field. But, thank God, there is another side to the picture, and this time the colors are white and gold. The apostle John was banished to the isle of Patmos as a prisoner of the Emperor Domitian, but God's hand was in everything, and one day a door was opened in heaven and the throne of God was revealed.

> After this I looked, and, behold, a door was opened in heaven: and the first voice which I heard was as it were of a trumpet talking with me; which said, Come up hither, and I will show thee things which must be hereafter.

> And immediately I was in the Spirit: and, behold, a throne
> was set in heaven, and one sat on the throne.[13]

There follows the presentation of the four and twenty elders,
the four living creatures, and the worship offered to Him that
sat upon the throne. Then he continues:

> And I saw in the right hand of him that sat on the throne
> a book written within and on the back side, sealed with
> seven seals.
> And I saw a strong angel proclaiming with a loud voice,
> Who is worthy to open the book, and to loose the seals
> thereof?
> And no man in heaven, nor in earth, neither under the
> earth, was able to open the book, neither to look thereon.
> And I wept much, because no man was found worthy to
> open and to read the book, neither to look thereon.[14]

God is revealing to His servant the riddle of history. This book
symbolizes God's purpose with respect to the entire universe
throughout history, and concerning all creatures in all ages
and unto all eternity. The book contains not only the story of
man's failure and sin, but also the story of God's mighty redemptive purpose for all men. No wonder St. John wept when
no one was able to open the book! For if the book were un-
opened, it would mean that the divine purposes concerning
man's salvation would never be fulfilled; it would mean also
that there would be no ultimate triumph for believers, no
new heaven and earth, no eternal inheritance for the suffering
saints. "No man was able to open the book." In other words,
man is incapable of solving the problems of his history. Therefore all history is one vast riddle, a maze without explanation,
a tangled skein of threads without pattern or design. What
must be emphasized is that "no *man*" was able to open the

13Rev. 4:1, 2.   14Rev. 5:1-4.

book. If there is to be an answer, it must come from another source; and it does:

> And one of the elders saith unto me, Weep not: behold, the Lion of the tribe of Juda, the Root of David, hath prevailed to open the book, and to loose the seven seals thereof.
>
> And I beheld, and, lo, in the midst of the throne and of the four beasts, and in the midst of the elders, stood a Lamb as it had been slain, having seven horns and seven eyes, which are the seven Spirits of God sent forth into all the earth.
>
> And he came and took the book out of the right hand of him that sat upon the throne.[15]

Immediately everything is changed. Here is One who has the answer to history. Where "no man" was able to open the book — He, the Lion of the tribe of Juda, the Root of David, is able. He can supply the answer, for He Himself is the answer. And this He now proceeds to reveal. The Lamb is going to show what God's purposes have been from the beginning. There has been a book. There has been a master-plan. God has been working according to that plan in spite of the seeming ascendancy of evil. His throne is inviolate in the heavens. His will is sovereign. Therefore, "Weep not." God's plans are going forward and will be revealed as perfect. That is what we read here in this mighty chapter of the Revelation of Jesus Christ; and it is here that we turn from the biblical pessimism about man and his history to the thrilling biblical optimism concerning man and his salvation. There is One who is God's answer. He is the "Lion of the tribe of Juda, the Root of David." He is also "the Lamb slain from the foundation of the world."

So let us note what is stated here concerning the history of all mankind and the purposes of God in it.

[15]Rev. 5:5-7.

G

I

First, above all, the Bible declares that at the heart of history there was One who did not choose evil.

The long entail of sin is therefore broken. In the fullness of time God sent forth His Son, born in the royal line of David, bone of our bone and flesh of our flesh. In all points He was tempted as we are; yet He did not sin. He refused to capitulate to the powers of Satan. At the beginning of His earthly ministry He was led up of the Spirit into the wilderness to be tempted of the devil. He was tempted to use His God-given powers selfishly and for His own use; tempted to attract men to Himself by the use of spectacular and sensational means; tempted to come to terms with the world and its ways instead of uncompromisingly presenting the truth of God's perfect law of righteousness and holiness. All such temptations He rejected. And all subsequent temptations He equally overcame. He walked with God and chose the pathway of humility, sacrifice and love. He "did no sin, neither was guile found in his mouth."[16] Of none other has this been true. But He, the Sinless One, is "holy, harmless, undefiled, separate from sinners."[17] He honored the divine law of God and made it honorable. He was "conceived of the Holy Ghost in the womb of the Virgin Mary," and was thus sanctified that the generation might be pure and undefiled as would have been true before Adam's fall. By the same Holy Spirit He was kept pure through all His life and "through the [same] eternal Spirit [He] offered himself [upon the Cross] without spot to God."[18]

It is this One who comes and takes the book from Him who sits upon the throne. He does so by reason of His victory over sin; and by reason of the atonement that He made for sin.

[16]1 Pet. 2:22.　　[17]Heb. 7:26.　　[18]Heb. 9:14.

Though it be true that man universally has turned to evil, yet here is One who is altogether unique in that He never sinned. The designs of the evil one are therefore thwarted. The law of God is glorified here in the earth. He finishes the work which the Father gave Him to do. Is there sin and crime and cruelty and suffering and unrighteousness on earth? Yes! Yet, supremely, there is also holiness and light and life and love. And all this St. John now sees as the book is taken from the hand of Him that sits upon the throne. He sees One who has altered the entire course of human history because He refused to conform to its choice of evil. He is "without blemish and without spot"[19]; He "loved righteousness, and hated iniquity"[20]; He was "the Holy One and the Just"[21]; and He was able to say, "The ruler of this world is coming. He has no power over me."[22]

II

Moreover, this Sinless One *has* the key and *is* the key to history.

St. John wept much because no man was able to open the book. But then he saw this One who came and took the book from Him that sat upon the throne. What "no man" was able to do, the "Lion of the tribe of Juda" could do. History has a key, and the key is Jesus Christ. That was what St. John saw that day as he gazed upon the throne. Man is incapable of saving himself. Philosophers and teachers have tried from the beginning of time but they have all failed. By this revelation in heaven it is declared that they will always fail, for man can never overcome the evil within himself. He is bound as a slave by his sin and his propensity to evil. But here is One who has broken the sequence of sin in the human race — has

[19]1 Pet. 1:19.   [21]Acts 3:14.
[20]Heb. 1:9.   [22]John 14:30 (RSV).

opened up thereby a new way of life and hope and blessedness — and is able to explain the purposes of God and to fulfil them too.

This is the heart of the good news of the Gospel. Jesus Christ is God's answer to all the dilemma of history. He divides history. All that He is and all that He accomplished while on earth are the central points in the plan of God. He is presented as "the Lion of the tribe of Juda, the Root of David," because He is the One who was promised long centuries before His birth to the patriarchs and the prophets. All ancient history leads up to Him. "To him give all the prophets witness."[23] In Eden God promised that He would come, and when the time was ripe, He appeared. Though He was in the form of God, yet He laid this aside in order that He might be found in fashion as a man, might humble Himself, and "became obedient unto death, even the death of the cross."[24] The Cross is central in all His work. That is why He is presented here as "a Lamb as it had been slain." And nothing needs to be emphasized more by Christians as they testify to their Lord and Saviour than just this — what He did upon the Cross is the central point of all history. Leave the Cross out of your survey of history and there is no key. Leave Christ out of the record and there is no answer, no solution to the enigma of history. But see Him as He is, crowned with glory and honor and exalted to the right hand of God because of the victory He won for men on the Cross, and you see that there is no reason whatsoever for pessimism concerning man. God's plan for history has been fulfilled to the very letter in Christ. He is the transcendent One. He gives history meaning. He shows that good and not evil will ultimately triumph. He demonstrates that Love is at the heart of the universe — not Satan.

[23]Acts 10:43.   [24]Phil. 2:8.

All this we are told through St. John as the Spirit reveals to him the surpassing glory of Him who holds the whole world in His hand, even Jesus Christ, the Lamb slain from the foundation of the world, yet the Lion of the tribe of Juda, the Root of David.

III

Not only is Christ, the Sinless One, the key to history; He is also the Lord of history.

"God also hath highly exalted him, and given him a name which is above every name: that at the name of Jesus every knee should bow, of things in heaven, and things in earth, and things under the earth; and that every tongue should confess that Jesus Christ is Lord, to the glory of God the Father."[25] These words of St. Paul assist us as we interpret St. John's vision of the throne set in the heavens and the opening of the seals of the book by the Lamb of God. He alone is able to read the book and to open the seals. When He met with the disciples after His resurrection He told them, "All power is committed unto me in heaven and in earth."[26] This is what St. John saw. No man could open the book. But Christ can. Therefore is He Lord of all history. The destiny of the world is in His hands. He comes to judge the world in righteousness. He comes to show that evil is not victorious. It was overcome at Calvary. He comes to make manifest to all men that the will of God through all history has been unassailable and that all the powers of Satan have been unable to divert God the Father Almighty by one iota from His original intent. Christ is Lord of history, and nothing is going to be permitted to happen without His consent. It is He, and He alone, who will open the seals of history. It is He who will command judgment

[25]Phil. 2:9-11.   [26]Matt. 28:18.

and mercy at their appropriate times. It is He who will make an end of sin and restore the earth to its primal glory. He comes to reign forever and forever, and in His kingdom there shall no evil be found.

This means that all the efforts of man to work out the salvation of the world according to a merely human program are doomed to failure. Man, however, still harbors this pathetic illusion. But the Bible gives not a single breath of encouragement to such thinking. The Bible reveals only one Lord of history — and it is not narrow-mindedness which refuses to accept any other contestant to His throne. Christianity is by its very nature intolerant of other solutions; for it is the revealed truth and all other representations are therefore either false or incomplete. St. Paul declared to the Galatians that if any man preached any other gospel than that which was originally delivered to them, "let him be accursed."[27] He is sounding the note of the true intolerance of vital Christianity. Intolerance like this is an essential element in the true religion. Intolerance like this can alone give adequate comprehension of what the Christian really is. When we have the only Gospel, and not till then, we have the Gospel for all.

Therefore, we proclaim Him Lord of all history. He and none other may hold the sceptre and the crown.

> Crown Him the Lord of peace,
>   Whose power a sceptre sways
> From pole to pole, that wars may cease,
>   Absorbed in prayer and praise;
> His reign shall know no end,
>   And round His pierced feet
> Fair flowers of Paradise extend
>   Their fragrance ever sweet.

[27]Gal. 1:8.

He came and took the book and, as He did so, the hosts of heaven upraised the cry: "Thou art worthy to take the book, and to open the seals thereof: for thou wast slain, and hast redeemed us to God by thy blood out of every kindred, and tongue, and people, and nation; and hast made us unto our God kings and priests: and we shall reign on the earth."[28] Christ is the answer. His hand is on the controls. His kingdom is forever.

IV

But there is yet one final word to be spoken. Christ, the Sinless One, the key to history, the Lord of history, is meantime calling out to Himself a people for His kingdom.

He has been doing this from the dawn of history. God has been continually choosing men for His kingdom. He marked them and drew them to Himself. He used them. He spoke through them. And Christ is calling a people to Himself today, a people who will turn from their sin and cleave unto righteousness, even as He Himself did. They will be a people who will trust in Him and in His blood shed on the Cross. They will be a people indwelt by His Holy Spirit and trained unto godliness and holiness. They will overcome by the blood of the Lamb and the word of their testimony. The will of God will be their delight. Communion with God, Father, Son, and Holy Spirit, will be their only joy.

In this people, the power of sin will be broken. Against this people, all hell will be unable to triumph. They have become "partakers of the divine nature, having escaped the corruption which is in the world through lust."[29] This world is not their home, for they "look for a city which hath foundations, whose builder and maker is God."[30] Already they dwell within that

[28]Rev. 5:9, 10.   [29]2 Pet. 1:4.   [30]Heb. 11:10.

city, for through adoption and sanctification of the Holy Spirit they "are come unto mount Zion, and unto the city of the living God, the heavenly Jerusalem."[31]

Christ fills all the horizons of His people. Their life becomes a life of service in His kingdom and for His glory. By the might of His grace, sin no longer has dominion. They are a people cleansed and made holy, humble and meek. And they look for the coming of the Saviour, the King of kings, and the Lord of lords, the Lion of the tribe of Juda, the Root of David, the Lamb slain from the foundation of the world, and the bright and morning Star.

[31]Heb. 12:22.

CHAPTER SEVEN

THE CROSS — GOD'S ANSWER TO EVIL

As there is only One God so there can be only one Gospel. If God has really done something in Christ on which the salvation of the world depends, and if He has made it known, then it is a Christian duty to be intolerant of everything which denies, ignores, or explains it away. The man who perverts it is the worst enemy of God and men; and it is not bad temper or narrow-mindedness in St. Paul which explains his vehement language in Galatians 1:8; it is the jealousy of God which has kindled in a soul redeemed by the death of Christ a corresponding jealousy for the Saviour. Intolerance like this is an essential element of the true religion. It is when we have the only gospel, and not till then, that we have the gospel at all.

James Denney in *The Death of Christ*

AT THE HEART OF history is the Cross of Christ. In 1825, when Sir John Bowring was Governor of Hongkong, he took a trip to Macao, and saw there a great bronze cross upreared against the sky, the last enduring monument of a cathedral which Portuguese traders had built long years before. A violent typhoon had struck the cathedral and left nothing but the front wall on which the cross had been upraised. It was the sight of this enduring emblem that inspired the hymn,

> In the cross of Christ I glory,
>   Towering o'er the wrecks of time;
> All the light of sacred story
>   Gathers round its head sublime.

The Cross abides. And to the riddle of evil, sin and suffering, the Cross of Christ is the answer of the Christian faith. Here the unsearchable and unanswerable Godhead is the victim of all the enormous and calculated fury of the powers of darkness and of evil. Here we see the kind of world which evil creates — a world that can accomplish the crime that killed the Man of Sorrows. Here indeed is the wreckage of time, sin-spawned, evil-dominated, demon-possessed. But here, too, is the unvanquishable love of God, giving God's best in return for man's worst, commending His love towards sinners in the hour of their greatest sin, and holding outstretched to the farthest limits of the world the wounded hands of love.

When Paul wrote to the Corinthians, he said, "I delivered unto you first of all that which also I received, how that Christ died for our sins according to the Scriptures."[1] For Paul, as for all the other apostolic writers, the Cross is the weightiest article of the faith of the Christian, the universal symbol of the Christian message, the center and the circumference of the Gospel. The preaching and the teaching of the New Testament center on the Cross. The Cross determines ultimately our concept of God, of man, of nature, of history and of eternity. It is the Christian's answer to the problem of suffering as well as of sin. For twentieth-century man, therefore, as well as for men of every age, the attraction and repulsion of the Christian faith are concentrated at one point — the Cross. Apart from Calvary, we have no clue to the maze. But at the Cross, God shows us both our sin and also the lengths to which eternal love will go to save us.

The Cross is God's answer to evil. The love of God is of such a magnitude, it suffers sin to reach its ultimate and itself accepts the suffering such an ultimate dictates; yet at the same time, by bearing the penalty which sin demands, love is victorious over it and can thereby grant to sinners everywhere the pardon of a great forgiveness.

How is the Cross the answer of God to evil? This question we must now study in depth.

The Bible calls moral evil by its own special name of "sin." The spirit and act of sin are in every form of hostility to the will of God. Sin expresses itself in folly and vice, in tyranny

[1] Cor. 15:3.

and oppression, in ambition and ruthlessness, in selfishness
and slavery, in dishonesty and iniquity, in moral perversity and
demonic activity, in anger and envy, in sloth and lust, in corruption and misgovernment, in transgression of God's law and
in enmity to the divine will. The Bible exposes the sin of man
on every page. It declares that this is a universal condition.
"The Lord looked down from heaven upon the children of
men, to see if there were any that did understand, and seek
God. They are all gone aside, they are all together become
filthy: there is none that doeth good, no, not one."[2] This is
the biblical diagnosis of man. "All we like sheep have gone
astray; we have turned every one to his own way."[3] Sin insinu-
ates itself through the doorway of the life of every man. Moral
evil indwells the human heart like a festering sore, and begets
things in its own image — suffering, pain, tears, groans, and
wretchedness and inhumanity to man. Sin carves a cross in
every life, and it was such sin which crucified the Lord of glory.
"They crucified him." This is the nadir of moral evil. You and
I live in a world so full of evil that it condemned incarnate
love. This world gave sentence against its Creator — "Crucify
him."

The historicity of the Cross is emphasized by the statement
of the creed — "He suffered under Pontius Pilate." It is no accident that Pilate is brought into the creed like this. It had to
be made abundantly clear that the passion of Christ does not
take place in heaven, or on some remote planet, or even in the
realm of ideas. The Cross happened in time, in the center
of the world history in which our lives are played out. We
are born into a world which is so evil, that when God sent
His Son into the world to dwell with men, they knew Him not,
they had no place for Him, they refused to listen to the word

[2]Ps. 14:2, 3.   [3]Is. 53:6.

He spoke to them about God, and finally they condemned Him to death. And we need not try to avoid the implications of such an act by saying that it belongs entirely to the past. Mystically, yet really, the passion of Christ is forever present. We are of the same stuff as the men who spurned Him in the days of His flesh. The spirit of the world has not changed. Horatius Bonar speaks for all men when he writes:

> 'Twas I that shed the sacred blood,
>   I nailed Him to the tree;
> I crucified the Son of God,
>   I joined the mockery.
>
> Of all that shouting multitude
>   I feel that I am one;
> And in that din of voices rude
>   I recognize my own.
>
> Around the cross the throng I see,
>   Mocking the Sufferer's groan;
> Yet still my voice, it seems to be,
>   As if I mocked alone.

The sins of Caiaphas and of Pilate are sins we see within ourselves. As in them, so in us are envy and malice and anger and pride. As they refused to listen to the Word of God when spoken by the Son of God, so have we refused. What happened in the judgment hall where Christ was so wrongfully condemned, is in reality the judgment of the hearts of all men everywhere: "We will not have this man to reign over us."[4]

The cruelty of the Cross must be noted too. Crucifixion was a form of execution devised by the Phoenicians and was described by Cicero as "crudelissimum et teterrimum" — the cruellest and the most terrifying of all departures from life. No Roman citizen

[4]Luke 19:14.

was ever allowed to die in this manner. It was a death reserved by the Romans for slaves and the like. Scourging always preceded crucifixion, undoubtedly to hasten death. The victim then bore the cross-beam to the place of execution, marching through the city streets in the company of the executioners. Once on the cross, the victim had nothing further done for him; he was left to die either of strangulation or of starvation. A stupefying drink was sometimes given to help deaden the pain, which was always intense, especially at hot seasons of the year. The strained position of the body, added to the insufferable thirst, caused the wounds from the great nails to strain and swell; the arteries of the stomach and head became surcharged with blood causing an intense throbbing of the head; this was usually followed by convulsions which tore the wounds further apart and left the victim a terrible object of suffering for all to see; cases were known of the suffering continuing for as long as thirty and forty hours before unconsciousness came and eventually death.

By His death, therefore, upon the Cross, our Lord entered into a form of suffering altogether beyond our imagining. He suffered pain at the hands of his fellows and did so as an innocent person. "I find in him no fault at all"[5] — that was the judicial verdict of Pilate's court. The trial was a mockery. He was guilty of no crime. Thus He came to His suffering on the Cross without cause — an innocent person led to the most terrible form of death ever devised by the mind of man. He was bound, blindfolded, spat upon, mocked at and scourged. "He is despised and rejected of men; a man of sorrows, and acquainted with grief. . . . He was oppressed, and he was afflicted, yet he opened not his mouth. . . . He was cut off out of the land of the living."[6] Thus Isaiah poignantly anticipates and foretells His suffering. All that

[5]John 18:38.   [6]Is. 53:3, 7, 8.

the evil imaginations of a sinful world could devise, He endured. He had done nothing but good. He had healed the sick, cleansed the leper, raised the dead. He had given sight to the blind, hearing to the deaf and speech to the dumb. He had taught with authority, and they had wondered at the gracious words which proceeded from His mouth. He had fed the hungry and had shown compassion to all men. Yet they crucified Him. Can anything more evil than this be conjured up? No wonder that Dr. Stalker, thinking of this and trying to analyze the psychology of the men who encompassed this crime, writes:

> There are terrible things in man. There are some depths in man in which it is not safe to look. It was by the very perfection of Christ that the uttermost evil of His enemies was brought out. As He now came into close grips with Satan, whose works He had come to destroy, the evil one exhibits all his ugliness and discharges all his venom through men. The claw of the dragon was in His flesh and its foul breath was in His mouth. "They spat on Him." It is impossible for us to conceive what such an insult must have been to His sensitive and regal mind.

This is the choice man makes at the heart of history. He chooses Barabbas, a murderer, in place of Christ, the Son of God. Aryan and Semite, East and West, are joined together in this foul deed. The searchlight of God here reveals the true essence of sin, and the radical bias of the human heart towards evil and away from the good. This stark awareness comes to Bishop Lancelot Andrewes as he meditates in his private devotions on the sufferings of his Lord:

> *Thou who didst design that Thy glorious head should*
> * be wounded:*
> *Forgive thereby whatsoever by the senses of my head*
> * I have sinned;*
> *That Thy Holy hands should be pierced:*

Forgive thereby whatever I have done amiss
By unlawful touch, or unlawful act;
That Thy precious side should be opened:
Forgive thereby whatever I have offended
By lawless thoughts in the ardor of passion;
That Thy blessed feet should be riven:
Forgive thereby whatever I have done
By the means of feet swift to evil;
That Thy whole body should be extended:
Forgive thereby whatever iniquity I have committed
By the help of any of my members.
And I too, O Lord, am wounded in soul;
Behold the multitude, the length, the breadth, the depth
* of my wounds;*
And by Thine, heal mine.

It is at the Cross that the promise of forgiveness is given. For the suffering of Christ was more than passion; it was action. He Himself had said, "I lay down my life. . . . No man taketh it from me, but I lay it down of myself. I have power to lay it down, and I have power to take it again. This commandment have I received of my Father."[7] Here is the incredible paradox of Christianity: God uses the very worst in man to reveal the greatness of His love. "God so loved the world, that he gave his only begotten Son."[8] Gave . . . ? It is *to the Cross* that God gives His Son. "He was delivered up," says Peter on the day of Pentecost, "by the determinate counsel and foreknowledge of God."[9] The Cross is no afterthought of God. Christ was "the Lamb slain from the foundation of the world."[10] Calvary is the place where the love of God is proclaimed in all its length and breadth and depth and height.

[7]John 10:17, 18.   [9]Acts 2:23.
[8]John 3:16.   [10]Rev. 13:8.

H

God is love. That is the story which we read in every paragraph of every page of the Bible. "He that loveth not, knoweth not God; for God is love."[11] Love is an essential attribute of God; and what that love is like we may learn from the other attributes of God which the Scriptures reveal. God is self-existent; therefore His love had no beginning. God is eternal; therefore His love can know no end. God is infinite; therefore His love can have no limits. God is immutable, and so His love cannot change. God is the Father Almighty, and we therefore acknowledge His love to be a vast, shoreless sea far, far beyond the scope of man's loftiest eloquence to describe or worthily portray.

God reveals His love. He does so in creation, for creation is a free act of sovereign grace. He does so in the ebb and flow of history, breaking in at decisive points to give direction and provide redemption. He does so in all His dealings with His chosen people, giving to them the gift of His law, His word through the prophets, and finally His very presence in Jesus. Christ moved among men, and wherever He went He radiated the love of God. He healed the sick and had compassion on all men, and in this He showed the good will of God towards all men. "Come unto me, all ye that labor and are heavy laden, and I will give you rest."[12] That was the call of God Himself, the call of a love whose riches are unsearchable. It was the love of God that spelled out the plan of salvation for sinners. The love of God is such that it refuses to let sinners go. Where sin abounded, there God's grace abounded. When sin entered the human race, the love of God moved against it inexorably.

> *Stronger His love than death and hell,*
> *Its riches are unsearchable;*
> *The first-born sons of light*

---

[11] 1 John 4:8.   [12] Matt. 11:28.

> *Desire in vain its depths to see;*
> *They cannot tell the mystery,*
> *The length and breadth and height.*

And it is this love that we meet on Calvary's hill. Here two tides meet — the tides of evil and the measureless ocean fullness of the love of God. In a sermon preached in 1750, the Rev. John Mac-Laurin, minister at Luss and the Ramshorn Kirk in Glasgow, Scotland, speaks in moving tones of the glory of the love that was seen at the Cross:

> God's love to His people is from everlasting to everlasting; but from everlasting to everlasting there is no manifestation of it known, or conceivable by us, that can be compared to this. The light of the sun is always the same, but it shines brightest to us at noon. The Cross of Christ was the noontide of everlasting love: the meridian splendour of eternal mercy. There were many bright manifestations of the same love before; but they were like the light of the morning which shines more and more unto the perfect day; and that day was when Christ was on the Cross, when darkness covered the land.

This is the measure of the love of God. He sends the everlasting Son to die in the place of sinners, making Him to bear vicariously the burden of human guilt, and thus to become the Mediator between God and man, the Captain of our salvation and the great High Priest who ever liveth to make intercession for His own.

The Bible exhausts itself in attempting to express the wonder of Christ's work upon the Cross. He is the ransom for many. "The Son of man came not to be ministered unto, but to minister, and to give his life a ransom for many."[13] His blood is the ransom price whereby sinners bound in their sin are set free. "Christ hath redeemed us from the curse of the law, being made a curse

---

[13]Matt. 20:28.

for us."[14] There is plentiful redemption in the shed blood of
Christ. Blind unbelief alone can limit it. He is "the propitiation
for our sins: and not for ours only, but also for the sins of the
whole world."[15] We are reminded by this of the ark of the
covenant over which was the mercy seat which was called the
propitiation.[16] The mercy seat was "the covering" or "the propitiation," indicating God's readiness to cover sin and to pardon the
sinner. At the Cross, Christ became our propitiation, the ground
and foundation on which God could vindicate His righteousness,
yet pardon sinful men. God is immutable, and therefore His
righteousness can under no guise be compromised. But the love
of God is such that it devises a way whereby love itself becomes
the foundation of a righteous justification of the sinner. Mystery?
It is altogether mystery. But glory? Yes, indeed!

> 'Tis mercy all, immense and free,
> For, O my God, it found out me.

A work of reconciliation is also fulfilled at the Cross. "You that
were sometimes alienated and enemies in your mind by wicked
works, yet now hath he reconciled in the body of his flesh
through death, to present you holy and unblamable and unre-
provable in his sight."[17] By dying as He did, bearing the sin of
the world and its judgment upon Him, Christ removed forever
the hostility of a holy God against sin already judged. There is
no need for a retrial of the sinner who accepts Christ as His substitute. And when the Holy Spirit touches our heart to see the
wonder of the love that brought the Saviour from the heart of
heaven to die on Calvary, then our innate hostility to God is
taken away and we find ourselves loving Him who first loved us.
"Calvary is the meeting place of Lovers," says the learned and

14Gal. 3:13.   16Ex. 25:21, 22.
151 John 2:2.   17Col. 1:21, 22.

scholarly St. Bernard. God and man are reconciled. Deity can alone meet the claims of deity. And it is this we see at Calvary where "God was in Christ, reconciling the world unto himself."[18] He takes our place. Christ forces Himself past us in order to become our "Substitute" at the Cross. He died "instead of" us. "In my place condemned He stood — bearing shame and scoffing rude." Thus He purchases our pardon with His most precious blood and opens for all who will believe the gates of the kingdom of heaven.

Thus the Cross is God's answer to evil. It is His answer to Satan — the evil one. The lifting up of Christ upon His Cross meant the casting down of Satan. "Now is the judgment of this world," our Lord said as He neared Calvary, "now shall the prince of this world be cast out. And I, if I be lifted up from the earth, will draw all men unto me."[19] It was "through death," we read in Hebrews, "that he destroyed him that had the power of death, that is, the devil."[20] Sin is judged at the Cross and the dominion of sin can be rejected by all who cleave to the Saviour of Calvary. It may not be possible for us to express the doctrine of the atonement in a way that will satisfy everyone — witness the classic soteriologies of the Church where Luther and Zwingli, Athanasius and Augustine, Calvin and Aquinas, all make different emphases. Yet in every one, Christ is seen as the only offering for sin. It is always the offended One Himself, the holy God who is of purer eyes than to behold iniquity, who Himself bears the sin of the sinner, and thereby opens a fountain for sin and for uncleanness, which is the only way to Paradise.

The New Testament affirms that the death of Christ was a cosmic necessity if sin were ever to be purged away from the universe of God. The deep heaven itself must be purged with the blood of a sacrifice greater than that ordained by Moses —

[18]2 Cor. 5:19.   [19]John 12:31, 32.   [20]Heb. 2:14.

and this would be none other than the sacrifice of Christ upon His Cross. Of this John Cordelier, the Roman Catholic mystic, writes in *The Path of Eternal Wisdom:*

> Behind the vesture of nature and of art, behind religion, knowledge, beauty, love in its myriad forms — we are to see this Creative Chivalry enduring to the utmost. Here is unsearchable and absolute Godhead, stripped of its vestments, wrung with agony, reduced to weakness in our interest, sparing itself nothing if thereby our souls may have more light.

Then he adds these vibrant words:

> If the Cross be anything at all it is the ground-plan of the universe. It stretches from nebula to nebula linking the farthest limits of the worlds, holding out to them the wounded hands of love.

This is the message that the Bible affirms in all its glory. Love reigns from the deadly tree. The Cross of Christ is the deathblow to evil of every kind and form. "Non victus sed Victor" — the ancient words thrill the heart as they declare again that Christ is not vanquished but victorious. Easter confirms the triumph and attests that light and not darkness, life and not death, good and not evil, God and not Satan, are at the foundation of all creation.

> *Jesus lives! thy terrors now*
>   *Can, O death, no more appal us;*
> *Jesus lives! by this we know*
>   *Thou, O grave, canst not enthrall us.*
>
> *Jesus lives! for us He died;*
>   *Then, alone to Jesus living,*
> *Pure in heart may we abide,*
>   *Glory to our Saviour giving.*
>
> *Jesus lives! our hearts know well*

Nought from us His love shall sever;
Life nor death, nor powers of hell
Tear us from His keeping ever.

It is at the Cross that all this is established finally and forever. The conflict, foreseen from all eternity by the Holy Trinity, is fought at the Cross. Here is the arena where the powers of darkness and the Christ of God meet for the final assault. Behind the Cross we may see all the massed legions of Satan and of hell aiding and abetting mankind in its endeavor to cast out the Prince of Life. "This is the heir; come, let us kill him."[21] Sin is the setter of the pace. Sin selects the weapons to be used. Sin erects the Cross and God sets His love upon the Cross, commending His love to us in that "while we were yet sinners, Christ died."[22] But God takes sin and uses it as the mightiest instrument of our redemption. God gives His best to us in response to and in terms of our worst. And from the conflict, love emerges victorious. Evil and all its forces are scattered and left in disarray. This is the victory of God. This is the death knell of evil. The Body broken on the Cross will become the Bread of Life to all who receive it. The Blood of the Son of God will become the elixir of eternal life to all who drink of it. It is His own word — the word of a Conqueror: "Whoso eateth my flesh, and drinketh my blood, hath eternal life; and I will raise him up at the last day. For my flesh is meat indeed, and my blood is drink indeed. He that eateth my flesh, and drinketh my blood, dwelleth in me, and I in him."[23]

This is the secret that dwells at the heart of life. This is the Word that is from everlasting to everlasting. Christ is victor at the Cross. To trust in Him is to prove His victory through every day.

[21]Luke 20:14.   [22]Rom. 5:8.   [23]John 6:54-56.

CHAPTER EIGHT

THE NEW CREATION — JUDGMENT AND REDEMPTION FROM EVIL

It is said, "To him that overcometh I will give a white stone, and in the stone a new name written, which no man knoweth saving he that receiveth it." What shall we take this secrecy to mean? Surely, that each of the redeemed shall forever know and praise some one aspect of the divine beauty better than any other creature can. Why else were individuals created, but that God, loving all infinitely, should love each differently?

C. S. Lewis in The Problem of Pain

Ye are come unto mount Zion, and unto the city of the living God, the heavenly Jerusalem, and to an innumerable company of angels, to the general assembly and church of the firstborn, which are written in heaven, and to God the Judge of all, and to the spirits of just men made perfect; and to Jesus the mediator of the new covenant, and to the blood of sprinkling, that speaketh better things than that of Abel.

Hebrews 12:22, 23, 24

In our study of the biblical answers to the problem of evil, we have seen that God permitted evil to enter His creation; we have seen that God allowed Satan to wage war against the saints, to test them; and we have seen, too, how God suffered the evil one together with evil men to encompass the Prince of Life in His death upon the Cross. But all this is only for a season. The Bible is one vast promise of the ultimate overthrow of evil. The judgment of a holy God on sin is certain. To the study of this divine judgment and what will be thereafter we must now turn.

There are many passages of the Bible at which we might begin; but the third chapter of St. Peter's second letter is as good a starting place as any. The apostle writes to comfort the Christians who have been finding it hard going by reason of many trials, and in doing so he points to the end of history and the new heavens and earth that are to be. "Nevertheless," he says, "we, according to his promise, look for new heavens and a new earth, wherein dwelleth righteousness."[1] This is the hope that he holds before them. "But, beloved, be not ignorant of this one

[1] 2 Pet. 3:13.

thing, that one day is with the Lord as a thousand years, and a thousand years as one day. The Lord is not slack concerning his promise, as some men count slackness; but is long-suffering to us-ward, not willing that any should perish, but that all should come to repentance. But the day of the Lord will come as a thief in the night; in the which the heavens shall pass away with a great noise, and the elements shall melt with fervent heat, the earth also and the works that are therein shall be burned up."[2] Evil, then, will have its day — but its day will end. A time will come when God will say "Enough," and from the throne the messengers of judgment will speed upon their way. St. Peter's is no isolated statement. The same note is heard through all the Scriptures, and any reading on the problem of evil that refuses to face this part of the divine revelation would be only a partial and a darkened answer.

"We look for new heavens and a new earth, according to his promise" — that is the apostolic affirmation. Our Lord taught likewise. "Verily I say unto you, That ye which have followed me, in the regeneration when the Son of man shall sit in the throne of his glory, ye also shall sit upon twelve thrones, judging the twelve tribes of Israel."[3] Now here we have a most interesting word — "the regeneration." It means "when everything shall be made new." Our Lord is pointing on to a day when He shall be revealed in all His glory, and in that day all things will be totally renewed. It will be a complete regeneration, an absolute rebirth, the present heaven and earth having passed away and a new heaven and a new earth with righteousness at its heart established forever. St. Paul is thinking of the same glorious events when he says that "eye hath not seen, nor ear heard, neither have entered into the heart of man, the things that God hath prepared for them that love him."[4] A like note is given in

[2] 2 Pet. 3:8-10.   [3] Matt. 19:28.   [4] 1 Cor. 2:9.

the sermon of St. Peter recorded in Acts, chapter three: "Repent ye therefore, and be converted, that your sins may be blotted out, when the times of refreshing shall come from the presence of the Lord; and he shall send Jesus Christ, which before was preached unto you: whom the heaven must receive until the times of restitution of all things, which God hath spoken by the mouth of all his holy prophets since the world began."[5]

In yet another passage from Romans — chapter eight — and we keep returning to this passage — St. Paul writes that "the whole creation groaneth and travaileth in pain together until now.... The creature itself also shall be delivered from the bondage of corruption into the glorious liberty of the children of God."[6] The emphasis is the same. Evil dominates the creation around us. Sin and suffering and pain have entered and infected the entire human race with thorns and briars, corruption and death, the hallmarks of such sin. From this infection no one is immune. God, however, has covenanted that there will be a complete overthrow of everything that is evil and that "new heavens and a new earth, wherein dwelleth righteousness" will yet be seen. The book of Revelation provides the climax. Here we see the Paradise that was lost in Eden restored again. The power of the serpent that encompassed the fall of man in Genesis is finally mastered in the Revelation of St. John, and "that old serpent, called the Devil, and Satan, which deceiveth the whole world,"[7] is cast into the lake of fire. In Genesis, we see man fleeing from God because of his sin; but in the book of Revelation the tabernacle of God is with men. God dwells with them and is their God. What was lost is restored. What was destroyed is remade. Through disobedience fellowship with God was broken. But now the gates of Paradise swing open to all believers, and the

---

[5]Acts 3:19-21.   [6]Rom. 8:21, 22.   [7]Rev. 12:9.

Tree of Life is accessible and given as God's greatest boon and blessing.

> I saw a new heaven and a new earth: for the first heaven and the first earth were passed away; and there was no more sea.
>
> And I John saw the holy city, new Jerusalem, coming down from God out of heaven, prepared as a bride adorned for her husband.
>
> And I heard a great voice out of heaven, saying, Behold, the tabernacle of God is with men, and he will dwell with them, and they shall be his people, and God himself shall be with them, and be their God.
>
> And God shall wipe away all tears from their eyes; and there shall be no more death, neither sorrow, nor crying, neither shall there be any more pain: for the former things are passed away.
>
> And he that sat upon the throne said, Behold, I make all things new. And he said unto me, Write: for these words are true and faithful.[8]

"I make all things new." That is God's promise. In the third chapter of his second letter St. Peter affirms this promise with fresh vigor. "Nevertheless we, *according to his promise,* look for new heavens and a new earth, wherein dwelleth righteousness."[9] He says also — with deep significance — that this promise has been made through the mouth of all the holy prophets since the world began. The regeneration of all things will be no afterthought of God. From the first of time, and indeed from ageless counsels of eternity, the triune Godhead has planned it so. Evil was allowed to enter. God in His sovereignty and wisdom ordained it so. God will use even evil for His glory. He will yet make the wrath of men to praise Him.[10] It has, however, no ultimate place in God's scheme. It is destined for destruction. Its overthrow is sure.

[8]Rev. 21:1-5.   [9]2 Pet. 3:13.   [10]Ps. 76:10.

This is no pietistic escapism. This is the truth of God, real as God is real. This is why St. Paul can say, "I reckon that the sufferings of this present time are not worthy to be compared with the glory which shall be revealed in us."[11] Without this note of triumph, the Christian faith would lack its ultimate vindication. The joys of heaven must be put in the scales against the sufferings of earth. The awesome destructiveness and corruption of moral evil must be viewed against the background of this divine revelation that they are only for a time and then will cease forever. We have no really Christian answer to the problem of evil without this kind of compensation. The transcendent holiness, righteousness and justice of God are at stake in this issue, and without the total overthrow of evil the sovereignty of God could not be assured. The answer of all the holy prophets since the world began is one with the affirmations of "the holy apostles" who were themselves taught by the Lord after His resurrection of "things pertaining to the kingdom of God."[12] Heaven's sun will yet rise upon a world that knows no sin. The last word will be with God — with the God whose name is, from everlasting unto everlasting, unutterable, holy love.

Now St. Peter develops this theme in the closing page of his second letter. He makes his bold and uncompromising assertion that judgment is going to fall on this sinful world with a perfectly clear mind, aware that many will mock at such preaching. Then he proceeds to outline the crisis point of world history which will usher in "the new heavens and the new earth" and concludes with a summons to all believers to live their lives from day to day in the light of this tremendous and momentous event — summons them to lives of holiness and dedication to their Lord and God.

[11]Rom. 8:18.   [12]Acts 1:3.

I

There will be a *continuity of unbelief*. St. Peter forewarns his readers of this. "There shall come in the last days scoffers, walking after their own lusts, and saying, Where is the promise of his coming?"[13] Now there are many things that we may say about a statement like this — perhaps, above all, that it is one of the most reassuring statements in all the Bible. For it demonstrates very clearly that the Scriptures are remarkably accurate in their prophecy of the course that history would follow. Every age has had its own quota of unbelief; this continuity of unbelief is a unique confirmation of the accuracy of biblical prophecy. The Bible nowhere says that the world will get better and better. It declares, on the contrary, that "evil men and seducers shall wax worse and worse, deceiving and being deceived."[14] Our Lord actually asked His disciples this question: "When the Son of man cometh, shall he find faith on the earth?"[15] Obviously, He did not look for any mass movement of mankind towards Himself. The course He foresaw for His Church was one of tribulation and persecution, their preaching rejected and their witness denied. "Then shall many be offended," He said, "and shall betray one another, and shall hate one another. And many false prophets shall arise, and shall deceive many. And because iniquity shall abound, the love of many shall wax cold. But he that shall endure unto the end, the same shall be saved."[16] Clearly our Lord saw that unbelief would spill over from age to age and that the latter end would be the worst of all.

It is clear, therefore, that the Christian should not be surprised at the unbelief of his generation. Our Lord has told us that the secularization of society will continue apace throughout history. Why should we then express amazement at such things?

[13] 2 Pet. 3:3, 4.
[14] 2 Tim. 3:13.
[15] Luke 18:8.
[16] Matt. 24:10-13.

They are the fulfilment of prophecy. This is what St. Peter is making clear to his hearers in his letter — scoffers will come denying the return of the Saviour; they will stubbornly refuse to accept the fact of divine revelation, which is so clearly stated, concerning creation and the flood that God sent upon creation. "They deliberately ignore this fact,"[17] he says. In other words, it is with absolute deliberation and set intent that they refuse to listen to the words of Scripture. The whole story of God's dealings with men has been clearly spelled out in the sacred records; but they deliberately refuse to believe them. They are ignorant of them willfully. As Paul writes in Romans, "[They] hold down the truth in unrighteousness."[18] That is what we see on every hand today. In the philosophies of the twentieth century there is no place for any eschatological intervention of God to close off history. Everything is expected to continue as it has always done. The stories of creation and the stupendous judgment of the flood are dismissed as mere myth. Likewise, the plain words of our Lord, that He will come again to judge the world in righteousness, are dismissed summarily without even the courtesy of reflection.

How shall the Christian react to this? With deep, deep thankfulness to God for telling the truth. The course of history is substantiating to the letter the biblical prophecy — thus strengthening the Christian's confidence in the Word of God. We must expect this continuity of unbelief in our times — and to the end of time. We must expect, though we deplore it greatly, that the apostasy from the faith will grow and spread. Every age has had its scoffers — and ours has plenty, too. You find them at every level of culture — in the arts and sciences, in the business board room and on the union picket line, in the universities and seminaries as well as in the smut production lines and the salacious advertising studios. "There shall come scoffers in the

[17]2 Pet. 3:5 (RSV).   [18]Rom. 1:18.

I

end time." The words of the apostle should nerve us for the battle of the faith even as they confirm our faith more deeply. Let men mock at the promise of "new heavens and a new earth, wherein dwelleth righteousness." God's word remains. The truth of the Lord shall endure forever.

> *Blind unbelief is sure to err*
> *And scan His works in vain:*
> *God is His own Interpreter,*
> *And He will make it plain.*

Unbelief spreads, rejecting God and mocking at the thought of judgment and a returning Christ. It is now as it was in the beginning. But God has told us that it would be so, and we can therefore with greater boldness place all our confidence in Him.

II

The apostle as he writes of the new creation has something to tell us about *the chronology of God.*

"But, beloved," he says, "be not ignorant of this one thing, that one day is with the Lord as a thousand years, and a thousand years as one day." That is a very remarkable statement. It shows that God is not bound by time as we are. God created time; but He is above time. Nonetheless, He works in time, using the time processes for the revelation of His will, though often the prints of His feet on the road of human history are centuries apart. It was "in the fullness of time" that God sent forth His Son. It was "in due time" that Christ died for the ungodly.

God has a timetable, but not one set by years and months and days and minutes. God's righteous acts in history are determined not by dates but by moral conditions. We must never forget that eternal Love is dealing with the waywardness of sinners and that everything Love can do to save the sinner from the error and evil of his ways will be done. Mercy and judgment meet together here. "The Lord is not slack concerning his promise, as some men count slackness; but is long-suffering to us-ward, not willing that any should perish, but that all should come to repentance." Here is part of the reason for the seemingly long delays of God. He is providing ample opportunity for repentance. All that love can do to woo men from their sin is being done. But clearly this cannot go on forever. There comes a time when the cup of iniquity is full to the overflow, and then God moves in judgment. "The heavens and the earth, which are now, by the same word are kept in store, reserved unto fire against the day of judgment and perdition of ungodly men."[19] Why this reservation? Why this delay? Because God is not willing that any should perish — therefore He waits. But not forever. We see this very clearly in Genesis, chapter six, where in verse 3 we read, "My Spirit shall not always strive with man"; and in verse 5 the reason for this is given: "God saw that the wickedness of man was great in the earth, and that every imagination of the thoughts of his heart was only evil continually. And it repented the Lord that he had made man on the earth, and it grieved him at his heart." Here is the clue to our understanding of the chronology of God. The hour of His judgment is determined by moral conditions on the earth. We read in Genesis 15:16 that "the iniquity of the Amorites was not yet full." So divine intervention is postponed. In other words, God waits to the last moment. He gives a sinning world every opportunity to turn to repentance. But a point of no return is evidently reached when judgment is inevitable — and that point arrives when the world's sin has itself reached the point of self-destruction. Then the hands upon the clock of God are really at the midnight hour. Then even God must cry, "Enough!"

It is in this light that we should understand our Lord's words:

[19] 2 Pet. 3:7.

"Jerusalem shall be trodden down of the Gentiles, until the times
of the Gentiles be fulfilled. . . . And then shall they see the Son
of man coming in a cloud with power and great glory."[20] Here
again is the same note — the fulfilment of the times of the
Gentiles, a time when the iniquity of the age will reach the
overflow point and judgment will fall. This is our age. This is the
Gospel age in which the good news of the love of God is
"preached unto the Gentiles." During this age, even while men's
sins accumulate and become ever more aggravated and corruptive,
the lamp of God's mercy burns and forgiveness is freely offered
to all who truly repent of their sins and place their sole confidence in Christ as Saviour and Lord. This is the wonder of the
everlasting mercy of God. It is unfailing, gracious, longsuffering,
tender, solicitous, compassionate, forgiving. The Holy Spirit still
strives with men, convicting them of sin, of righteousness and of
judgment. But even this will end. "The day of the Lord will
come as a thief in the night; in the which the heavens shall pass
away with a great noise, and the elements shall melt with fervent
heat, the earth also and the works that are therein shall be
burned up."[21]

Who shall stand in that day of wrath? They only who are
hidden in the Rock of Ages. They shall not be afraid when
fear cometh.

III

The *totality of evil's overthrow* is also specially noted here. It
will be awesome, sudden, overwhelming and final.

We have seen that God permitted evil to enter creation and
that Satan was granted permission to continue operating among
men — testing, tempting to evil, prompting to sin and in general

[20]Luke 21:24, 27.   [21]2 Pet. 3:10.

working out his fell will. We have seen that, under the direction of the evil one, men encompassed the Prince of Life in His death upon the Cross. We have seen, too, that evil has continued to grow with ever-increasing intensity until now. But evil will have its end. The world in which we live will not be allowed to continue forever under the dominion of the devil. And so we read:

> The heavens and the earth, which are now, by the same word are kept in store, reserved unto fire against the day of judgment and perdition of ungodly men.
> The day of the Lord will come as a thief in the night; in the which the heavens shall pass away with a great noise, and the elements shall melt with fervent heat, the earth also and the works that are therein shall be burned up.

This the apostle repeats with redoubled emphasis:

> [This will be] the coming of the day of God, wherein the heavens being on fire shall be dissolved, and the elements shall melt with fervent heat.[22]

In other words, the judgment will be total judgment. "All these things shall be destroyed." Peter stresses here that, even as the old world was destroyed by flood, so will our present world be destroyed by fire. Now that may seem ludicrous to the majority opinion of modern man. We well know that even within the Church there are many who have so far parted company with belief in the infallibility and inerrancy of the Scriptures that they can read these words with a big yawn. But why should this be? On what authority may any man, and more especially any man who makes profession of being a disciple of Jesus Christ, pick and choose from the full spectrum of biblical doctrines in order to form his own private system of belief? Since when has God abrogated or re-written any page of the New Testament?

[22] 2 Pet. 3:7, 10, 12.

The Scriptures still stand inviolate, all of them God-breathed, all of them written by "holy men of God, [who] spake as they were moved by the Holy Ghost."[23] The Word of God is our only rule of faith and life. And in this Word we read these solemn verdicts: "The wages of sin is death"[24]; "The soul that sinneth, it shall die."[25] The end of sinning is death and destruction. The end of evil is total overthrow, judgment and eclipse.

God would not be God if it were otherwise. A righteous and holy God demands that righteousness be vindicated in the overthrow of evil; and when God's Word says that God's judgment is going to be demonstrated in the heavens passing away with a great noise and the earth with the works therein being burned up, who is man to gainsay or to argue with his Creator? Here indeed is a very simple test of a true Christian. Do you believe this Word of God or do you not? If the Scriptures give a false directive here, how can we be sure that they are right elsewhere? "All Scripture is given by inspiration of God"[26] — and it is high time that we stop being evasive and accept the divine Word as saying what it means and meaning what it says. Christian eschatology is as true as any other part of Christian truth. Moreover, the emphasis of this chapter is agreed to and supported by all other sacred writers. Their testimony is uniform and undivided. It is with unfragmented unanimity that they declare that the day of the Lord will come and that in that day the final overthrow of evil will be consummated.

What is being said here is that God is going to destroy evil completely and to consume it by the breath of His mouth from His universe. We are told that "all these things shall be dissolved . . . the heavens shall melt with fervent heat . . . and the earth also and the works that are therein shall be burned up."

23 2 Pet. 1:21.　　　25 Ezek. 18:4.
24 Rom. 6:23.　　　26 2 Tim. 3:16.

Nothing could be more clear. Nothing could be more absolute. Sin shall be no more. God has said it and the Word of the Lord endureth forever.

I do not know whether this world as we know it will be completely destroyed, whether God will fashion a new one altogether. There has been much debate on this. In the natural order as we know it, nothing is ever completely destroyed by fire; and it may well be that, even as the generation of Noah was completely destroyed by the flood yet the same earth remained, so will it be after the flame of God's purification has passed across this globe. All that defiles will be burned out. The earth as we know it — this sinful, sinning earth — will be destroyed. Then either what remains will be a new earth, or nothing will remain at all. Whatever God's pattern of working may be, this much is sure. A new earth will arise from the ashes of the old — and in that new earth God will begin to work out His new purposes of grace.

IV

Some hints are given by St. Peter of *the glory of this new creation*. It will be a new heaven and a new earth, "wherein dwelleth righteousness."

Think of it. Everything of sin will have been burned out by the fire of divine judgment and all that sin has wrought will be banished forever. It is questionable whether even the memory of it will remain. If God is able to cast our sins behind His back and to remember them no more, is it beyond imagining that His people may be granted a like faculty of complete forgetfulness of a sinning past? We dare not dogmatize. But this is His promise — a world without thorns and briars, a world without pestilence and disease, a world without suffering and pain, a world without perversity and without perversion. It is impossible for us even to imagine what this will be like. All we are told is that "eye hath not seen, nor ear heard, neither have entered into the heart of man, the things which God hath prepared for them that love him."[27] We see now only as in a glass darkly when we contemplate these glorious things. But that it will be glorious and breath-taking is beyond doubt. Everything will be different. Color will be different. We have literally no idea what color will be like in the new creation. Beauty and perfection will appear and be rejoiced in. Earth's animals will be different; the lion and the lamb will lie down together. Infinite day will exclude the night and pleasure will banish pain.

For that day, as St. Paul reminds us, "the whole creation groaneth and travaileth together in pain until now . . . waiting for the manifestation of the sons of God."[28] The travail will not be in vain. Out of a cleansed heaven the sun will shine upon a purified earth. Then indeed Paradise will be regained. This will be "the regeneration" of which our Lord speaks, the restitution of all things to their primal glory — the glory which God originally intended that they should know. No longer will earth be "the silent planet," unresponsive to the voice of her Creator. Rather, all earth's thousand voices will lift to the heavens their songs of praise and all the sons of God will shout for joy. In that psalmody of praise there will be a recovery of all the harmonies we have sought for in this sinful earth — the melodies that have eluded us, the dreams that have faded when most we longed to possess them. In the new creation we shall know as we are known and love our Saviour with unsinning heart.

Could anything be more majestic, grander, lovelier than this? And it is covenanted in promise. "We, *according to his promise*, look for new heavens and a new earth, wherein dwelleth righteousness."

[27]1 Cor. 2:9.   [28]Rom. 8:22, 19.

A new earth
made by God —
fashioned and framed
all new;
inhabited by people who
are glad in God
and love Him
with unsinning heart.

Its cities full of new creation:
fountains flowing love —
all work a joy,
and worship in it all;
with children playing
in the streets all day.

Mountains and plains
with colors unimagined;
fragrance from flowers
like incense
rising —
sunrise: but no sunset
and light perpetual.

Movement yet rest;
friendship — fulfilment;
homes that are simple
yet palatial,
Christ-planned and built —
and music, tingling sweet,
heard everywhere.

New heavens above,
new earth —
and God in all

> *men's thoughts*
> *and dreams.*

Thus will it be in the day of the new creation, when God will be all in all, and the knowledge of the Lord will fill the land as the waters fill the sea.

V

There we might end; but the apostle doesn't let us end there. He has something particular to say about *the purity of the lives of those who wait for this day.*

He refers to this frequently. In verse 11, "Seeing then that all these things shall be dissolved, what manner of persons ought ye to be in all holy conversation and godliness?"[29] He goes on, "Wherefore, beloved, seeing that ye look for such things, be diligent that ye may be found of him in peace, without spot, and blameless."[30] And further, "Ye, therefore, beloved, seeing ye know these things before, beware lest ye also, being led away with the error of the wicked, fall from your own steadfastness. But grow in grace, and in the knowledge of our Lord and Saviour Jesus Christ."[31]

The apostle regards the contemplation of the glory ahead in a very practical light. It must not leave us star-gazing; rather it should nerve us for the stern rigors of the daily road and quicken our pursuit of God who leads us only in the paths of righteousness. We are summoned by these vistas before us to holy living, to earnest watching, to faithful praying and to patient working. The words that we find here are words that mirror the fruit of the Holy Spirit — holiness, godliness, spotlessness, blamelessness, diligence, growth in grace, steadfastness against untruth. These are the marks of the Christian disciple who waits for his Lord.

[29] 2 Pet. 3:11.   [30] 2 Pet. 3:14.   [31] 2 Pet. 3:17, 18.

With such a blessed hope in view he sets himself to be as like his Lord as he possibly can. To that pure hope he presses, "with every grace endued." In this adulterous and sinful world, he loves God, the Father, the Son, and the Holy Spirit, and his neighbor as himself. This world is not his home. Within the fellowship of the Church he serves his Lord and "according to his promise, looks for new heavens and a new earth, wherein righteousness will dwell."

CHAPTER NINE

DAILY DELIVERANCE FROM EVIL

We seem to be left to the heartlessness of a thousand petty demons, who pervade every little circumstance; who seem, like the fabled Lilliputians, to tie our hands and feet while we sleep; who snap all the threads of our financial looms; who upset our ordinary plans; who turn anticipated joys into ashes. There are times when a current of such things sets in; times when everything seems to weave itself into a network of crippling environment, and any attempt to extricate ourselves only bruises us.

But it is in hours like these He speaks: "Fear not, I have redeemed thee, I have called thee by thy name, thou art mine." Testing is a proof of His love and confidence. Much trial and suffering mean that God has confidence in us; that He believes we are strong enough to endure; that we shall be true to Him even when He has left us without any outward evidences of His care.

He wishes us prepared for the highest services. Therefore He tests us in a thousand ways.

J. Gregory Mantle from *Beyond Humiliation*

"LEAD US NOT INTO temptation, but deliver us from evil."[1] Our Lord taught the disciples to ask for this. The Lord's prayer has many petitions — indeed it covers all the major aspects of our daily lives. It is a child's prayer, *Our Father;* a worshipper's prayer, *Hallowed be thy name;* the prayer of a soldier, *Thy kingdom come;* the prayer of a servant, *Thy will be done;* the prayer of a beggar, *Give us this day our daily bread;* the prayer of a sinner, *Forgive us our debts, as we forgive our debtors.* But the climax of all the supplications is reached in the cry for complete deliverance from evil. And rightly so. The Lord's prayer is to be prayed by people who still live in an evil world. Is there to be any total deliverance from evil? May we rightly expect to be freed from temptation and given an unbroken record of victory in the moral struggle? The answer is, We may. God does not teach us to ask for things that He cannot and will not give. Even now, in this present evil world, we may experience a full salvation — we may prove effectively that our Saviour is "able also to save them to the uttermost that come unto God by him."[2]

[1]Matt. 6:13.   [2]Heb. 7:25.

139

From evil, Lord,
deliver me,
as Thou hast promised to deliver
all
who cry to Thee.

Into temptation, Lord,
direct me not,
unless Thou there dost undertake
my soul to keep:
and from the fowler's snare,
from all the tempter's wiles,
his crafts and darts,
his snakish guiles
me victor
forth to bring.

Praise will I offer
then
when in the Spirit's power
I come again;
for in that hour of testing
I will prove
Thy resurrection life,
Thy power and love divine,
unconquerable.

From every evil, Lord,
from every sin,
deliver Thou my soul,
without,
within:
and in me now
Thy triumph show,

Thy victory declare;
Hear this my cry — and Thine —
O God,
attend my prayer.

Let it be emphatically affirmed that the Christian life is a divine life supernaturally begotten by the Holy Spirit, and supernaturally strengthened through the resurrection life of Jesus Christ. God intends that His people should day after day experience deliverance from evil: both from "moral evil," and from "the evil one" as well. It is the will of Christ that we live in the power of His resurrection. Therefore we can actually lead a life in which His promises are taken as they stand and are found to be true. We can actually cast all our care upon Christ and enjoy deep peace in doing it. We can actually have the thoughts and imaginations of the heart cleansed and kept pure moment by moment. We can actually enter into temptation and yet emerge as victor on the field. Christ is victor. That is the good news that thrills from every page of the New Testament. And in His victory His servants share. They experience a full salvation. Thoughts and desires and senses are kept purified moment by moment as the Holy Spirit raises us in Christ to life divine. Deliverance from evil is a reality — here and now.

We have already seen in Chapter Three that by divine permission Satan is allowed to test God's people. Such testing, however, is intended by God to become an opportunity for spiritual victory. Job was tested — but he emerged triumphant. Paul was tested in a host of ways, but one particularly: "There was given to me a thorn in the flesh, the messenger of Satan to buffet me"[3]; nevertheless, he came through triumphantly. He found that God's grace was sufficient. Temptation in itself

[3] 2 Cor. 12:7.

K

is not sin. We sin only when we yield to temptation; and that we need not do. Our Lord was tempted; but He sinned not. He was tempted under the sovereign direction of the Holy Spirit; indeed, we read that after His baptism in the river Jordan, "immediately the Spirit driveth him into the wilderness. And he was there in the wilderness forty days, tempted of Satan; and was with the wild beasts; and the angels ministered unto him."[4] The impression we get is that our Lord's temptation was "timed" by the Holy Spirit. He was *led* into temptation. Yes! But He was *delivered* from the evil. Luke tells us that "when the devil had ended all the temptation, he departed from him for a season. And Jesus returned in the power of the Spirit into Galilee: and there went out a fame of him through all the region round about."[5] It is for a like victory that we are taught to pray. We need not fall before the tempter. In every temptation, we may count on God to "deliver us from evil."[6]

But there are conditions to a life of spiritual victory. What are they?

I

First of all, we must resolve by God's grace to turn from all known evil.

This is fundamental. "Abhor that which is evil; cleave to that which is good."[7] For the disciple of Jesus Christ, no other choice is possible. Our Lord is our pattern here. He was "separate from sinners"[8]; and as is the Master, so should the servant be. He died to sin. He died rather than sin; and all who follow Him must follow Him in this "dying to sin."

True repentance begins here. Repentance is a change of

---

[4]Mark 1:12, 13.   [6]Matt. 6:13.   [8]Heb. 7:26.
[5]Luke 4:13, 14.   [7]Rom. 12:9.

mind concerning ourselves, concerning our sin, and concerning the Saviour. When through the illumination of the Holy Spirit we see ourselves as God sees us, and by the grace of the same Spirit begin to desire to "walk in newness of life,"[9] we experience a complete change of mind, especially about the nature and power of indwelling sin. Sin becomes distasteful. A godly sorrow over sin is given us, and we turn from our sin "to serve the living and true God."[10] Now, the more closely we walk with Christ, the more eagerly we desire to be like Him — and this means that we, with ever-increasing determination, resolve that sin will not reign "in our mortal bodies, that [we] should obey it in the lusts thereof."[11] Likewise, we reckon ourselves "to be dead indeed unto sin, but alive unto God through Jesus Christ our Lord."[12] From all known evil we turn. From everything that we know to be grieving to the Spirit of God we turn away. With Charles Wesley we pray,

> Ah! give me, Lord, the tender heart
> That trembles at the approach of sin;
> A godly fear of sin impart,
> Implant and root it deep within,
> That I may dread Thy gracious power,
> And never dare offend Thee more.

Perfect consecration to God, the Father of our Lord and Saviour Jesus Christ, involves a total renunciation of all we know to be evil.

But there are many who are unwilling to take such a step of absolute self-denial and rejection of sin. Many are like Augustine who in his earlier years would pray, "Lord, save me from my sins — but not yet." We want the blessing of spiritual

[9]Rom. 6:4.   [11]Rom. 6:12.
[10]1 Thess. 1:9.   [12]Rom. 6:11.

victory; but we are not prepared to meet God's conditions — the first of which is that we deliberately turn from sin. In this, however, God's standard is absolute. If spiritual victory is to be won, then sin must be put away. "Look for no peace within," writes John Wesley in his sermon on *The Wilderness State,* "till you are at peace with God which cannot be without 'fruits meet for repentance.' Is there outward sin of any kind? Does your conscience accuse you of committing any sin, whereby you grieve the Holy Spirit of God? Where these things are, God will depart from you, and joy and peace will depart with Him. And how can you expect that they will return, till you put away the accursed thing? 'Cleanse your hands, ye sinners.'[13] 'Put away the evil of your doings.'[14] So shall 'light break forth as the morning...and thy righteousness shall go before thee'[15]; '...return unto the Lord, and he will have mercy upon him; and to our God, for he will abundantly pardon.' "[16]

In utterly putting away sin, the penitent must not forget about his sins of omission. Whoever neglects the means of grace strays from God's ways and invites the assaults of Satan. "If thou dost habitually neglect any of the ordinances of God," says one of the Puritan preachers, "how canst thou expect that the light of His countenance shall continually shine upon thee?" Only the Holy Spirit can lighten our darkness in such things, and we must continually cry to Him for His help. His grace will enable us, however; if we are honest and sincere, He will show us where we fail and where we sin. To turn from all such sin will then become our duty and our joy. Repentance of this quality will be the first guarantee of victory over sin and of our being "delivered from evil."

[13]James 4:8.   [15]Is. 58:8.
[14]Is. 1:16.   [16]Is. 55:7.

II

Next, we must learn to rely continually on God.

This is how our Lord lived. "I can of mine own self do nothing: as I hear, I judge: and my judgment is just; because I seek not mine own will, but the will of the Father which hath sent me."[17] His life was a dependent life. "The Son can do nothing of himself, but what he seeth the Father do: for what things soever he doeth, these also doeth the Son likewise."[18] He came "to do the Father's will." He never wrought a miracle of Himself, as witness His words, "The works which the Father hath given me to finish, the same works that I do, bear witness of me, that the Father hath sent me."[19] He never spoke of Himself; His claim was always consistent: "My doctrine is not mine, but his that sent me."[20] So when we reach the great priestly prayer of St. John, chapter seventeen, it is fitting to hear Him pray, "I have glorified thee on the earth; I have finished the work which thou gavest me to do."[21] He maintained: "I must be about my Father's business."[22] At every level of His life and work there was a total reliance on God. He took the place of dependence which Adam refused to take. He disowned all power of a self-originating life. He trusted in God, and said: "As the living Father sent me, and I live because of the Father; so he that eateth me, he also shall live because of me."[23] The temptation in the wilderness was above all else an attempt to break this spirit of dependence upon God. Satan tried again and again to get Him to use His own powers. But He would not. His trust was in God alone, and not for a single syllable of recorded time was that confidence broken.

Now it is this spirit of dependence which we must cultivate

[17]John 5:30.
[18]John 5:19.
[19]John 5:36.

[20]John 7:16.
[21]John 17:4.
[22]Luke 2:49.

[23]John 6:57 (ASV).

if we would gain the victory over all evil. Independence of God is an evil thing. Self-reliance is an evil thing. Better to rely wholly and solely on God — this is the will of God which is truly good and acceptable and perfect. This kind of dependence makes it hard for Satan to reach us at a vulnerable spot. He will try, of course. His constant effort will be directed towards getting us into a mood of unfaith — into a place of self-dependence, that is; and if he ever succeeds in getting us there, then certainly we will go down before him. He may try also to get us to place our confidence in others — as he tried and succeeded all too often in tempting Israel to put her trust in foreign alliances rather than in God alone. But against all temptation there is one attitude which always succeeds — dependence upon God. David knew this. "In the time of trouble he shall hide me in his pavilion: in the secret of his tabernacle shall he hide me."[24] This was David's confidence. He had learned to rely on God and had proved Him in the great crises of life. Yet even David passed through times when he gave place to the devil and fell into grievous sin. There were times when he failed to watch and to pray; and bitter were the sorrows he knew as a result of such carelessness. Sin is a hard taskmaster. And each one of us may likewise fall. Our only safety is in constant reliance upon God. He alone can deliver us from evil. He alone can keep us in the evil day. He alone can deliver from the "pestilence that walketh in darkness; [and] the destruction that wasteth at noonday."[25] To rely on God is to possess the victory.

III

Again, we must equip ourselves to resist the devil.

We have already seen much of the work of "the enemy —

[24]Ps. 27:5.   [25]Ps. 91:6.

the evil one." He sows tares among the wheat. He tests and tries the children of God. He tempts to evil of all kinds. "Be sober, be vigilant; because your adversary the devil, as a roaring lion, walketh about, seeking whom he may devour: whom resist steadfast in the faith."[26] Thus St. Peter counsels the Christians to whom he writes; and it is out of bitter experience he speaks. His Lord had said to him, "Satan hath desired to have you, that he may sift you as wheat"[27]; and St. Peter had dismissed the warning, saying, "Though I should die with thee, yet will I not deny thee."[28] Thus he boasted. But within a few hours Satan broke through his guard and St. Peter denied his Lord with oaths and curses. He could not forget that day. How often must he have gone back over the tense events of these crowded hours and thought: "If only I had been more vigilant against the devil! If only I had been consciously aware of his demonic subtlety and kept close to the Lord!" But he was careless. He slept in Gethsemane. He joined himself to the wrong kind of company. And the devil got him — caught him at the point where he counted himself the strongest, and gained the advantage over him. In that dark hour, instead of being "delivered from evil" he was "delivered over to the evil one."

All this is written for our admonition. The Holy Spirit has thus seen to it that we should learn from the errors into which even the greatest saints have fallen. "Resist the devil," writes James, "and he will flee from you."[29] And St. Paul adds his word of counsel: "Put on the whole armor of God, that ye may be able to stand against the wiles of the devil."[30]

How shall we resist the devil? By turning from all evil, and by relying on God to keep us from falling; in such penitence and trust we have moved in the direction of spiritual victory.

[26] 1 Pet. 5:8-9. [28] Matt. 26:35. [30] Eph. 6:11.
[27] Luke 22:31. [29] James 4:7.

But we can be even more specific. We resist the devil when we refuse to place ourselves in the way of temptation. We resist the devil when we listen to the voice of the Holy Spirit whispering in our heart that danger is near. We resist the devil when in the hour of temptation we look away to Calvary and plead again the power of the blood of the Son of God. We resist the devil when we declare over and over again to ourselves that "Jesus Christ is Lord."[31] We resist the devil when, though knowing that we ourselves have no power to resist him, we nevertheless rely utterly on the victory of Christ, and so say to him, "The Lord rebuke thee."[32] We resist the devil also when we sing the songs of Zion in our hearts — one thing Satan cannot stand is the voice of praise and the sound of singing to the Lord. The psalmist so reminds us: "Let the high praises of God be in their mouth, and a two-edged sword in their hand ... to bind their kings with chains, and their nobles with fetters of iron."[33] Praise will "bind the strong man."[34] We resist the devil as well when we "abide in Christ" moment by moment and make diligent use of all the appointed means of grace — the Holy Scriptures, the power of prayer, the holy communion of the blessed sacrament. These all become hedges through which the evil one cannot penetrate; and when to all this we add the whole armor of God, as listed in the last chapter of St. Paul's letter to the Ephesians, we are equipped to foil the works of the devil and to abort his malicious design.

John Bunyan wrote *The Holy War* as an allegory: Satan captures the soul of man and Emmanuel ultimately triumphs over the devil. After Mansoul has been recaptured, many of the inhabitants of the city are put on trial — Mr. Hard-Heart,

[31]Phil. 2:11. [33]Ps. 149:6, 8.
[32]Jude 9. [34]Matt. 12:29.

Mr. Hate-Good, Mr. Incredulity, Mr. Lustings, and many more — and they are brought before the bar of justice where a jury is sworn in. How clear. Bunyan's genius makes the situation! The very names of the twelve jurymen are an index of the powers by which we may "resist the devil": "Mr. Belief, one; Mr. True-Heart, two; Mr. Upright, three; Mr. Hate-Bad, four; Mr. Love-God, five; Mr. See-Truth, six; Mr. Heavenly-Mind, seven; Mr. Moderate, eight; Mr. Thankful, nine; Mr. Humble, ten; Mr. Good-Work, eleven; and Mr. Zeal-for-God, twelve." Where such spirits rule within the heart of the believer, there is little room left for Satan to fill. Armed with such support, we shall truly "resist the devil." We may be led into temptation; but we shall most certainly be "delivered from evil."

IV

One final point. We must cultivate the communion of the Holy Spirit.

Our Lord promised His disciples: "I will pray the Father, and he shall give you another Comforter, that he may abide with you for ever."[35] As He saw how desolate they were at the thought of His leaving them, He added, "It is expedient for you that I go away: for if I go not away, the Comforter will not come unto you; but if I depart, I will send him unto you."[36] Then He told them of some of the things that the Holy Spirit would do. "When he, the Spirit of truth, is come, he will guide you into all truth: for he shall not speak of himself; but whatsoever he shall hear, that shall he speak: and he will show you things to come. He shall glorify me: for he shall receive of mine, and shall show it unto you."[37] Tenderly He spoke to them of the way in which the "other

[35]John 14:16.   [36]John 16:7.   [37]John 16:13, 14.

Comforter" would be with them in every situation, would guide them into all truth, and would empower them for every form of service. By the coming of the Spirit, they would be equipped unto every good work and strengthened for every ministry of grace. Pentecost fulfilled the promise. The Holy Spirit fell upon them, filled them, renewed them, spoke through them and glorified Christ in them and before their generation. Through the eternal Spirit, they were enabled to offer their bodies as living sacrifices and their members as instruments of righteousness unto God. They rejoiced in the wonderful "communion of the Holy Ghost."[38] They experienced the penetrating power of His love and grace. The Holy Spirit was One whom they loved and worshipped the same as the Lord Jesus Christ Himself. Day by day they claimed His power for holy living and fruitful service.

This was as it should be. This was what Christ had promised them. And it is this same experience that the Christian of the twentieth century must know if he is to overcome the evil around him and within him. We, too, may know in our times the miraculous penetration of the Holy Spirit — His entering into every faculty of our personality and making the mind of Christ apparent in us. We may not be able to offer any explanation as to how this takes place but we may, nonetheless, experience its truth and power. A near approach to an understanding of how the Spirit interpenetrates our personality may be borrowed from devotional teachers of some hundreds of years ago. When we place a piece of iron in a fire, they used to say, and blow up the coals, the heat gradually intensifies and soon the fire begins to penetrate the iron; so that in a brief time we have not only the iron in the fire but the fire in the iron. These two distinct substances interpenetrate

[38]2 Cor. 13:14.

one another, and that to a point where they almost become one.

So it is with the indwelling Spirit. He indwells the believer. And as He does so, He penetrates and fills our personalities in such a way that we become "one with God." In doing so, the Spirit is never alone, for the persons of the Godhead never work separately. All acts of God are done by all three persons. God never manifests Himself in one person without the other two. God is absolutely and altogether present wherever He is present.

But the particular office of the Holy Spirit is to make Christ real and to reveal His power and glory. To this end, the Holy Spirit indwells the heart of the believer and constantly works to show forth Christ therein. We cannot know Christ without the Spirit even as we cannot know the Spirit without knowing Christ. Likewise we cannot know the Father without knowing the Son. If, then, we are to "grow in grace and in the knowledge of our Lord and Saviour,"[39] we must cultivate the communion of the Holy Spirit. We must learn to "walk in the Spirit, and ... not fulfil the lust of the flesh."[40] We must constantly commit our way to the Holy Spirit — even as our Lord, "who through the eternal Spirit offered himself without spot to God."[41]

What this means is that we are delivered from evil as we allow the Holy Spirit to quicken us and to renew us in the image of Jesus Christ. By the empowering of the Holy Spirit we turn from all known sin. By the enlightening of the Holy Spirit we learn to acknowledge our daily sins of omission. Through the grace of the Holy Spirit we increasingly commit our way to God and trust in Him. It is only with the Spirit's aid that we are able to resist the devil. "We are the circumcision," writes St. Paul again, "which worship God in the spirit, and rejoice in Christ Jesus, and have no confidence in

[39]2 Pet. 3:18.   [40]Gal. 5:16.   [41]Heb. 9:14.

the flesh."[42] Here are the two elements of spiritual worship. The Spirit exalts Jesus and abases, annuls, overcomes the flesh. If we would truly glory in Jesus, and have Him glorified in us, if we would know the glory of Jesus in personal and unchanging experience, free from the impotence which always marks the efforts of the flesh, we must simply learn what this worship of God by the Spirit is — we must simply cultivate "the communion of the Holy Ghost."

Deliverance from evil comes from God — by His Spirit indwelling us and making Christ real in us. The same Spirit who raised up Christ from the dead, will also quicken us and lift us into a life of fellowship with God the Father through Jesus Christ the Son. This, and nothing less than this, is the destiny of God's children here and now. This is the heritage of the saints through the marvelous grace of a God whose name is love. "The law of the Spirit of life in Christ Jesus hath made me free from the law of sin and death."[43]

And how may we prove this? How may we be sure of it? Let some words of Dr. Andrew Murray seal the sum of the matter:

> You must take your stand upon God's blessed Word. You must accept and appropriate His teaching. You must take the trouble to believe that God' means what He says. I am a temple; just such a temple as God commanded to be built of old. He means that I should see in that temple of old what He plans that I should be. In the temple, the holiest of all was the central point, the essential thing. It was all dark, secret, hidden, till the time of the unveiling came. It demanded and received the faith of priest and people. Likewise, within me, the holiest of all is hidden and unseen, a thing for faith alone to know and deal with. Let me, as I approach the Holy One, bow before Him in deep and lowly reverence. Let me there say that I believe what He says, that His Holy

[42]Phil. 3:3.   [43]Rom. 8:2.

Spirit, God, one with the Father and the Son, even now has His abode in me. I will meditate and be still, until something of the overwhelming glory of this truth breaks upon me, and faith begins to realize it. I am His temple. And in the secret place He sits upon the throne. As I yield myself to Him, day by day surrendering and opening up my whole being to Him, He will in His loving, divine, living power, shine into my consciousness the light of His presence.

This is the pathway to spiritual victory. This is the road that leads to daily deliverance from all evil.

Come then, let us resolve by God's grace to turn from all sin. Let us rely on the faithfulness and the power of Almighty God to keep us from falling. Let us refuse to allow the devil to have his way with us — resisting him with all the heavenly armory which Christ has supplied. And let us more and more rejoice in the communion of the Holy Spirit, knowing that He proceeds from the Father and from the Son, and assured that it is His single and sovereign purpose to save us from sin and from the love of sinning, to preserve us daily from all evil, and finally at the last to present us faultless in the presence of God's glory with exceeding joy.

CHAPTER TEN

CONSTANT VICTORY OVER EVIL

We are more than conquerors through him that loved us.
Romans 8:37

One who never turned his back but marched breast forward,
Never doubted clouds would break,
Never dreamed, though right were worsted, wrong would
triumph,
Held we fall to rise, are baffled to fight better,
Sleep to wake.

Robert Browning from *Epilogue to Asolando*

Suffering is universal. In the language of every nation there is a word for pain; and instinctively we count pain an evil thing. Why should this be? Was Hitler right when he wrote in *Mein Kampf*, "Mankind has grown strong in eternal struggles and it will only perish through eternal peace"? Or is there a peace which can be known even in a sea of trouble, a peace which is a foretaste of the triumphant peace of heaven?

The answer of Christianity is unique and unmistakable. "God is our refuge and strength, a very present help in trouble."[1] And Jesus Christ on the eve of Calvary said to His disciples, "Let not your heart be troubled."[2] God's promise to His children is the gift of an untroubled heart. As the Scottish paraphrase says,

> *Let troubles rise, and terrors frown,*
> *And days of darkness fall;*
> *Through Him all dangers we'll defy,*
> *And more than conquer all.*

Spiritual victory is possible over the evil that lurks alongside suffering. Undoubtedly, Satan will employ every technique

[1]Ps. 46:1.   [2]John 14:1.

L   157

in the hope of shattering our faith. But the Christian need not falter, need not fall.

> Nor death, nor life, nor earth, nor hell,
> Nor time's destroying sway
> Can e'er efface us from His heart,
> Or make His love decay.

All this God promises — all this and heaven, too. "He hath said, I will never leave thee, nor forsake thee. So that we may boldly say, The Lord is my helper, and I will not fear."[3] Therefore, we affirm that God never allows His people to suffer without good reason; and that suffering, when it comes, opens up the possibility of new discoveries of the greatness of God. It is the Christian's destiny to experience constant victory over evil.

Now, St. Paul has much help to offer in this great debate. Only occasionally does he unbare his heart and tell us of some of the suffering he endured; but the first chapter of his letter to the Corinthians is such an exception. There we learn how deep were the waters through which he passed. "We would not, brethren, have you ignorant of the trouble which came to us in Asia, that we were pressed out of measure, above strength, insomuch that we despaired even of life: but we had the sentence of death in ourselves, that we should not trust in ourselves, but in God which raiseth the dead."[4] Clearly, he knew what suffering was — the dark days heavy with pain; the long nights filled with suffering, loneliness and bewilderment. Writing of this, he says very simply to the Corinthian Christians that in the darkness he put God to the test and found that His encouragements were adequate for all the troubles of every day. But more than that, he found that every detail of the suffering had meaning. "This means," he says, "that if we

[3]Heb. 13:5, 6.   [4]2 Cor. 1:8, 9.

experience trouble we can pass on to you comfort and spiritual help; for if we ourselves have been comforted we know how to encourage you to endure patiently the same sort of troubles that we ourselves have endured."[5]

Yes, indeed! Life's troubles become the arena for God's encouragements. The apostle goes on:

> We are quite confident that if you have to suffer troubles as we have done, then, like us, you will find the comfort and encouragement of God.[6]

It is very evident as we read on into the chapter that St. Paul is referring to some great crisis point in his life. He doesn't go into as much detail as we should like. He keeps to the very broad outlines of his problem; but even these are sufficient to show that he plumbed the depths of extreme suffering and actually was near to death. J. B. Phillips translates the mood as well as the words of the apostle very accurately:

> At that time we were completely overwhelmed; the burden was more than we could bear; in fact we told ourselves that this was the end.[7]

One cannot go much further than that. Here is suffering, trial, testing and obviously terrifying pain. Yet he goes on to say:

> Yet we believe now that we had this experience of coming to the end of our tether that we might learn to trust, not in ourselves, but in God who can raise the dead.[8]

The sentence of death was in his mortal body. He had borne all that he could humanly bear. Then God did something new for him — gave him back his ministry and encouraged him to share with others all that he had learned and proved of God in the darkest hours of his weakness and pain. The encourage-

---

[5] 2 Cor. 1:6 (Phillips).   [7] 2 Cor. 1:8 (Phillips).
[6] 2 Cor. 1:7 (Phillips).   [8] 2 Cor. 1:9 (Phillips).

ments of God never failed. His grace sufficed to the end. And all this happened for two great reasons: one, that he should cease trusting in himself; and two, that he should become a means of encouragement and inspiration to others.

Note here the great elements of the grace of God. No matter what form the evil may take — sudden bereavement, business disaster, bodily illness, nervous breakdown or family tragedy — it provides an opportunity of proving the promises of God and of putting them to the test. If we are walking in the will of God, such tests will come only by His appointment and with grace at their heart. And if perchance we are walking contrary to His will, then trials of this kind only come in order to pull us back to His side.

This is the meaning and the message of verse ten:

> [He] delivered us from so great a death, and doth deliver: in whom we trust that he will yet deliver us.[9]

Past, present and future are all alike covered by the gracious providence of our heavenly Father. He will never take us into the battle without guaranteeing to us the victory at the last. This is His promise. Speaking of the sparrows on the rooftops, He has said,

> Not one of them shall fall on the ground without your Father.[10]

St. Luke renders the same promise in these words:

> . . . not one of them is forgotten before God.
> But even the very hairs of your head are all numbered. Fear not therefore: ye are of more value than many sparrows.[11]

What an insight into the heart of God! He sees each sparrow fall. He knows the pain of the animals of His creation, the pain man creates for God's creatures and the pain they inflict

[9]2 Cor. 1:10.   [10]Matt. 10:29 (ASV).   [11]Luke 12:6, 7.

on themselves. God knows it all. Even this lesson, however, is taught to us in order that we might more firmly believe that God cares for His people, cares for and watches over them through every variety of mortal experience. Nothing ever happens that cannot be God's instrument of blessing. God can still roll great stones away and make them seats for angels. His mercy is from everlasting to everlasting. He knows our frame and never forgets that we are dust.

> *Things future, nor things that are now,*
> *Nor all things below or above,*
> *Can make Him His purpose forego,*
> *Or sever my soul from His love.*

This is the hope of the Christian. Because of this we can confidently say that by the graciousness of an Almighty God, we may know constant victory over evil.

Everything, however, must be kept in perspective, and there are certain facts which we must not forget.

I

Pre-eminently, we must note that *God has not promised His children exemption from pain.*

Suffering was Paul's lot — as it was the lot of so many of the apostles and prophets.

Dr. H. W. Frost in *Miraculous Healing* summarizes something of the sufferings which the saints have undergone. Much of this comes to us, of course, by tradition; but it is an interesting indicator of what faith in Christ implied and to what it most generally led. He writes:

> Matthew suffered martyrdom by the sword in Ethiopia. Mark died at Alexandria after being dragged through the streets of the city. Luke was hanged on an olive tree in Greece. John was put in a cauldron of boiling oil but escaped death

and was banished to Patmos. Peter was crucified at Rome with his head downwards. James was beheaded at Jerusalem. James the Less was thrown from a pinnacle of the temple, and beaten to death below. Philip was hanged against a pillar in Phrygia. Bartholomew was flayed alive. Andrew was bound to a cross, whence he preached to his persecutors till he died. Thomas was run through the body at Coromandel in India. Jude was shot to death with arrows. Matthias was first stoned and afterwards beheaded. Barnabas was stoned to death by the Jews at Salonica. Paul was beheaded by Nero at Rome.

So the grim record runs on. The saints of God suffer. The sufferings of Job have become proverbial, and rightly so, for Job is typical of the suffering of the people of God. With cruel mockings and imprisonment, with scourging and bonds, they testified to their unshakable faith in the righteousness of God. As the writer of the epistle to the Hebrews reminds us,

> Others had trial of cruel mockings and scourgings, yea, moreover of bonds and imprisonment:
> They were stoned, they were sawn asunder, were tempted, were slain with the sword: they wandered about in sheepskins and goatskins, being destitute, afflicted, tormented;
> Of whom the world was not worthy: they wandered in the deserts, and in mountains, and in dens and caves of the earth.[12]

In the providence of the God in whom they trusted, pain was their lot. For them, there was no special exemption from suffering.

The same was true of our Lord. We have already seen that He was made "perfect through sufferings."[13] And He very plainly told His servants that in following Him they would not be given any special deliverance from hardship or persecution. "In the world ye shall have tribulation,"[14] He told them. Indeed,

[12]Heb. 11:36-38.   [13]Heb. 2:10.   [14]John 16:33.

there is a special beatitude reserved for those who suffer for righteousness' sake. "Blessed are ye, when men shall revile you, and persecute you, and shall say all manner of evil against you falsely, for my sake. Rejoice, and be exceeding glad: for great is your reward in heaven: for so persecuted they the prophets which were before you."[15]

This being so, we must stubbornly refuse to entertain any suggestion that when a Christian suffers, it is a sign of some lack of faith on his part, an evidence that he is out of touch with God. One frequently hears the saying that all sickness comes from Satan and may be refused by faith. How errant can men be! Suffering may well be a sacred trust — a sign of honor among the elect of God. Let it be granted that in the beginning pain was the effect of sin. Let it be accepted that had there been no sin, there would have been no suffering. Let us concede that Satan directs suffering under the permissive will of God; the grand drama of Job certainly supports such a view. But none of this means that if we suffer, it is through our lack of faith; or that if we exercise sufficient faith, healing is certain and deliverance sure. Nothing could be further from the biblical revelation. Nowhere is there promised to the believer complete exemption from pain. The contrary is the case. God still permits Satan to attack us through thorns in the flesh. But this can be for the eternal good of our souls. "It is a blessed fever," says Samuel Rutherford, "that summons Christ to the bedside." Elsewhere, as he meditates on the same theme, he adds,

> I hope you are not ignorant, that if peace was left to you in Christ's testament, the other half of the testament was a legacy of Christ's sufferings. For did He not say that pain would be our lot? "These things I have spoken unto you,

[15]Matt. 5:11, 12.

> that in me ye might have peace; in the world ye shall have
> tribulation."

Truth speaks in these lines. Suffering is not an elective of the
Christian. We are not promised exemption from it. But when
it comes, it must be regarded as another token of God's trust
in us.

> *By hand unseen*
> *This soul was led*
> *Into the place of pain;*
> *So strange it seemed*
> *That this must be*
> *God's path, to joy and gain;*
> *And yet, I learned*
> *Within the fire*
> *How precious He can be*
> *Unto the soul*
> *That walks alone,*
> *That will not go out free.*

This is the biblical revelation. All else is falsehood and error.
The first condition of victory over the evil that lies at the
heart of suffering is a clear recognition that God knows what
is best for us. In such acceptance of the will of God lies peace.

II

To this we must add another wonderful truth. *God goes
with His children as they undergo pain.*

One of the loveliest of all names for God is "the God of
all comfort."[16] It was in such a light St. Paul had come to
know the Father of mercies. He "comforteth us in all our tribu-

---

[16] 2 Cor. 1:3.

lations."[17] In every trial God was near. Isaiah had proved this centuries before:

> I will mention the loving-kindnesses of the Lord, and the praises of the Lord, according to all that the Lord hath bestowed on us, and the great goodness toward the house of Israel, which he hath bestowed on them according to his mercies, and according to the multitude of his loving-kindnesses.
>
> For he said, Surely they are my people, children that will not lie; so he was their Saviour.
>
> In all their affliction he was afflicted, and the Angel of his presence saved them: in his love and in his pity he redeemed them; and he bare them, and carried them all the days of old.[18]

Yes, that is what God does. When His people undergo trial, He promises to be with them.

> When thou passest through the waters, I will be with thee; and through the rivers, they shall not overflow thee: when thou walkest through the fire, thou shalt not be burned; neither shall the flame kindle upon thee.[19]

Thus are God's children upheld. He is with them. He is with them to comfort, that is, to strengthen them. He is the God of all comfort and the upholder of all who call upon Him.

One could give countless illustrations. A letter came to me a few days ago from one who was entrusted with grievous sickness and for months lay helpless in the hospital. For weeks she lay almost totally unconscious and of this she said, "The coma in which I lay for so long was as it were the shade of His hand upon me." Juliana of Norwich, saint and mystic, in her remarkable book *Revelations of Divine Love* tells of the day when deep darkness fell on her: "At the end of it, all was dark, and I saw no more. As a wretched creature I moaned and cried for feeling of my bodily pains, and for failing of

[17]2 Cor. 1:4.   [18]Is. 63:7-9.   [19]Is. 43:2.

comfort, spiritual and bodily. But then suddenly there came to me a word which was spoken clearly and mightily. It was my Lord who spoke; and He said not, Thou shalt not be tempested; but He said, Thou shalt not be overcome." Samuel Rutherford, too, of whom we have already spoken, knew much of the upholding of the Lord he served; and on the trials through which he passed, he made this comment:

> When we shall come home and enter into the possession of our Brother's fair kingdom, and when our heads shall feel the weight of the eternal crown of glory, and when we shall look back to the pain and suffering of time; then we shall see life and sorrow to be less than one step or stride from a prison to glory; and then our little inch of time suffering will not be worthy of our first night's welcome home to heaven.

This is what Job learned. There were so many things in his experience which he could not understand. He went backward and forward, to the right and to the left, seeking an explanation; but it always eluded him. Still his faith in God remained unshaken. He was convinced that God knew what it was all about and that his trials were for his ultimate good. God was with him. He was sure of it. Therefore he said, "He knoweth the way that I take: when he hath tried me, I shall come forth as gold."[20]

Our Lord has told us how He will comfort and strengthen us. This is the special office of the Holy Spirit, the Comforter. "I will pray the Father, and he shall give you another Comforter, that he may abide with you for ever."[21] When St. Paul speaks of being comforted by the God of all comfort he uses the same word the Lord used when addressing the disciples in the upper room. The Comforter, the Holy Spirit, indwells the life of the believer and brings the resurrection power of

[20]Job 23:10.   [21]John 14:16.

Christ to his aid. So God is real in every situation. His help
is real, His word is real. His Spirit upholds and strengthens for
every discipline and constantly makes Christ Jesus precious and
truly present. So in every hospital bed, on every battlefield, in
every malaria-infested jungle, in every domestic crisis, in every
temptation, the Holy Spirit glorifies Christ and the believer is
enabled to say: "I will fear no evil: for thou art with me."[22]

III

Then, too, *God uses pain, to our blessing and to His glory.*
St. Paul emphasizes this. Admittedly, there are many things
that are far beyond our mortal understanding. Sometimes our
Lord spoke about suffering being to the glory of God, but
He never said how. Nowhere in all the Scriptures is there a
definite explanation of trial. God's children are trusted with the
unexplained.

Nevertheless, when the apostle bares his heart about his own
suffering, he shows to us some of the ways in which God uses
pain.

For one thing, God uses pain to make us trust Him more.
"We had the sentence of death in ourselves," Paul writes,
"that we should not trust in ourselves, but in God which raiseth
the dead."[23] What happens is that God often brings us to the
very end of our tether, in order to reveal Himself to us as the
God of resurrection. He knocks away all the props of our life.
He takes from our side those in whom we have relied. He
brings us down into the valley of bitterness. But there is purpose in it all, namely, to teach us to trust Him completely. For
we are so naturally prone to self-confidence, self-trust, self-
obeisance. The old nature within us, the old carnal nature of
trust in self and doubt of God, dies hard. Men as we are, we

[22]Ps. 23:4.   [23]2 Cor. 1:9.

are proud and cocksure. Then God sends suffering. God permits Satan to buffet us. He brings us very low. Why? Only that we might trust Him more and more — and come to know Him as He is, the God who is alive, the God of resurrection, the God who has life in Himself.

But more than that, God uses pain to train us in the great ministry of comforting others. St. Paul stresses this here. "Experience shows that the more we share Christ's suffering, the more we are able to give of his encouragement."[24] How true that is! Who can comfort like one who has himself passed through like problems and pain? The experience of trouble enables us to pass on spiritual comfort to others. God wants us to be like Himself; and since He is the God of all comfort, He wants us to be comforters too.

Amy Carmichael makes this striking distinction in *Edges of His Ways*. "Sorrow is one of the things that are lent," she says, "not given. Joy is given; sorrow is only lent. Sorrow is lent to us for just a little while that we might use it for eternal purposes. Then it will be taken away and everlasting joy will be our Father's gift to us. So let us use this *lent thing* to draw us nearer to Christ; and let us use it to make us more tender to others." One who learned this lesson in the school of pain has written of it and left these lines:

> *Humbly I asked of God to give me joy,*
> *To crown my life with blossoms of delight;*
> *I begged for happiness without alloy,*
> *Desiring that my pathway might be bright;*
> *Tearful I sought these blessings to attain —*
> *But now I thank Him that He gave me pain.*
>
> *For with my pain and sorrow came to me*

[24] 2 Cor. 1:5 (Phillips).

A dower of tenderness in act and thought;
And with the suffering came a sympathy,
An insight that success had never brought;
Father, I had been foolish and unblessed,
If Thou hadst granted me my blind request.

The ministry of the Christian disciple is one of comfort. The touch of a loving hand, the welcoming smile of kindness, the Christ-given ability to sit where men sit — this is our task; and God uses suffering to equip us for it.

God uses pain also as a token of His trust. F. B. Meyer, saint and sufferer, once said: "Trials are God's vote of confidence in us." There is a profound reason for this. Suffering, when rightly accepted, becomes a participation in Christ's sufferings. That is what St. Paul says here: "The more we share Christ's suffering, the more we are able to give of his encouragement."[25] Now admittedly there is mystery here. How can we in any sense partake of the sufferings of Christ? Again, no complete explanation is given. But from the New Testament revelation it is clear that, in some divine way, we may in our suffering demonstrate to heaven and to hell the victory of Christ and the triumph of His resurrection. Everything depends on how we accept what God sends. To accept complainingly is to frustrate the high purposes of God. But to receive buffetings as a sacred trust and to bear them in the spirit of meekness and total reliance upon God, is to give assurance that the glory is Christ's — the victory in the suffering is Christ's victory. So God entrusts His child with sickness. He knows what He is doing. He goes before. He plans the way. He provides the succour. He sustains and helps in every need. He

[25]2 Cor. 1:5 (Phillips).

uses the suffering as a means of sanctifying our souls and bringing glory to His name.

IV

And *God delivers us from the evil at the heart of pain.*

For there is evil there. It is possible for the child of God to be broken by the pain. It is possible for the evil one to have the victory over us in the valley of the shadow. Suffering is a test, a stern and rugged test, and it can be exceeding grievous. We may easily fail.

God's will, however, is that we should overcome. If we do go down before the tempter, it will be because we have taken our eyes off our Lord. The promise of the Lord is complete deliverance in the evil day. And to this St. Paul gives witness. He "delivered us from so great a death, and doth deliver: in whom we trust that he will yet deliver us."[26] He makes the theme vibrant: "Our light affliction, which is but for a moment, worketh for us a far more exceeding and eternal weight of glory; while we look not at the things which are seen, but at the things which are not seen; for the things which are seen are temporal; but the things which are not seen are eternal."[27] This is Victory with a capital V. This is the victory which they inherit who trust in God forever.

We must never forget that every testing brings with it the possibility of defeat — but also the possibility of glorious victory. It is only of victory that the apostle speaks here, and rightly so; for God has supplied us with every provision against spiritual defeat. We need not fall. We serve a risen Saviour, and He is with us today and every day. He waits to be tested. He guarantees us complete victory over all evil when we trust Him only and put no confidence in the arm of our flesh. The

[26]2 Cor. 1:10.   [27]2 Cor. 4:17, 18.

will of God is that here on earth we prove the faithfulness of His promise and that here and now we experience by faith the blessedness of the life to come. In that life which is before us, suffering will be no more and every tear will be wiped away. God will be all in all and Christ the sole glory in Immanuel's land. To that hope we press "with every grace endued." In the triumphant anticipation of the hour when all mysteries shall be explained we "rejoice with joy unspeakable and full of glory."[28] This is "the victory that overcomes the world."[29] This is why we are "steadfast, unmovable, always abounding in the work of the Lord, forasmuch as [we] know that [our] labor [and travail] is not in vain in the Lord."[30] And this is why we constantly say, "Thanks be to God, which giveth us the victory through our Lord Jesus Christ."[31]

[28] 1 Pet. 1:8.
[29] 1 John 5:4 (RSV).
[30] 1 Cor. 15:58.
[31] 1 Cor. 15:57.

CHAPTER ELEVEN

POSTSCRIPT

Father, if He, the Christ, were Thy Revealer,
   Truly the First Begotten of the Lord,
Then must Thou be a Sufferer and a Healer
   Pierced to the heart by the sorrow of the sword.

Then must it mean, not only that Thy sorrow
   Smote Thee that once upon the lonely tree,
But that today, tonight, and on the morrow
   Still will it come, O Gallant God, to Thee.

Give me, for light, the sunshine of Thy sorrow,
   Give me, for shelter, shadow of Thy cross;
Give me to share the glory of Thy morrow,
   Gone from my heart the bitterness of loss.

Studdert Kennedy from The Suffering God

SOME TIME AGO I was guest preacher for holy week services in a town in northern Ontario and while there visited the local hospital one day with my minister host. In one room we met with an RCMP officer. He had been in an accident with the cruiser and was in great pain. He said to us: "I wish I knew why this has happened to me." It was hard to know what to say, but eventually I hazarded this: "You know, God has sometimes to put a man on his back in order to get a look at his face." More might have been said, but his pain demanded silence; so, with a handclasp, a smile, and a prayer, we left.

Life is like that. There is the usual routine of things. Everything is fine so long as all is well at home, or at work, or in the circle of one's family and friends.

Then something happens.

It may be sudden death. A friend's life is snuffed out in a pile-up on the thruway. It might be financial disaster. The finance company goes bankrupt and you were deeply involved. Illness can strike you down overnight — the searing pain that circles round the heart and down your arm or the mental break when your nerves were too taut — and you find yourself in a hospital bed looking at the ceiling: or, worse still, sitting on the edge of a bed in deep, deep depression and too frightened to talk to a soul.

Trouble takes many forms. A man comes home from work and finds a note from his wife saying she has gone and won't be back. A mother learns that her child has fallen into evil ways.

Some months ago I spent a night in California in the home of an elder in the church where I was to preach the following day. We went for a walk after supper, and on the way he told me something about the family.

"You saw the boys that we had supper with tonight?" he began. I nodded. One boy was twenty-one, the other eighteen.

"This is our family," he said; "my wife and I and those two boys. The boys mean everything to me and my wife. Well, one night two years ago, the boys went out in the Pontiac. About 10:30 the telephone rang. It was the police. 'Do you have a Pontiac, such and such a number?' they asked.

"'I do.'

"'Well,' they answered, "it has gone over the embankment, and there are two boys in it, and they are critically injured in the hospital. You'd better come right over.'"

We walked along, and after a moment my friend continued. "I went to the hospital; but they were both unconscious. I couldn't recognize their faces."

It is happening every day; every hour of the day. And it is so easy to become callous about it. Indeed, many people do. The shock of suffering seems to anesthetize the mind and make it incapable of turning in God's direction. Even when God uses the megaphone of pain, we are slow to hear, slow to obey.

Yet God is very close to a man when faced with disaster. He spoke, for instance, in the most personal way to my Californian friend as he stood by the side of his unconscious boys.

"Do you know," he said to me as we walked on, "it was there in the hospital as I stood by my boys that God spoke to me and said, 'Now! Will you be mine?' For years I had known what I ought to do with Jesus Christ. My wife had found the Saviour and she had witnessed to me and prayed for me; but I wouldn't yield. It was only when tragedy struck that God got through to me."

Yes! Some do respond immediately. They find God in the shadows and worship Him as Saviour and Lord.

What has Christ to say to anyone who gets caught in the clutch of pain? What have I, as a believer in Jesus Christ, to say to a sufferer who does not yet know the good news of the Gospel?

Many things. But some are vital. Let me mention a few of them.

First, I tell him that God can use the trouble as a means of revealing His grace. This He can always do. But we must give God His chance. He may have waited a long time to look us in the eyes, and we must lay our presuppositions and prejudices aside in order to let God have His own way in us. This means being absolutely honest with God, being open-minded and willing to listen to anything He wants to say.

Next, I remind him that Jesus Christ is love. He died for the sins of the whole world and died to provide a way of forgiveness for all who seek it. But He is raised from death; is exalted to the right hand of God; and by His Spirit is present everywhere to work the miracle of recreation of character and life. He is the Light of the world and can help me understand "the reason why" of the suffering; and since He is the Son of God with power, He can give me strength to bear the burden of any day.

Another thing to be said is this. Even under the assault of bitter grief or pain, Christ can so deal with my personality that

He gives me a spirit of compassion for others. And this is something that grows and grows and grows. He works within our selfish hearts and renews them in His own image, giving us love where there was hate, concern where there was only coldness, and strength where before only weakness was known.

This leads me naturally to say that the next step is one of simple, humble, eager prayer. Christ must be tested. We must try Him and see if He is true to the word of His promise. To pray is to use the pragmatic test of experience. Only the simplest words need be used in a prayer like this. It is the heart-cry that reaches Christ. So,

> *Speak to Him now, for He hears,*
> *And spirit with spirit may meet;*
> *Closer is He than breathing,*
> *And nearer than hands and feet.*

The answer to such eager, earnest prayer is always a miracle. God answers prayer. He does so in a million ways. Sometimes the answer is immediate. At other times it is delayed. But God's timing is best. No one ever called on Him without being heard and getting the right answer.

Here, then, is the conclusion of the matter for the present. I would add only that what I have written has been not only an exposition of the Holy Scriptures, but also an affirmation of my own deepest belief — a belief that has been tested in ways and through days that I am unable to describe. If there is one lesson, more than any other, that I have learned, it is this — God is utterly to be trusted. His footprints may be hard to trace, but the goal is unmistakable.

His faithfulness is beyond all doubt.

INDEX OF SCRIPTURE PASSAGES